THE NEW
CUNARD
QUEENS

THE NEW
CUNARD
QUEENS

QUEEN MARY 2
QUEEN VICTORIA
QUEEN ELIZABETH 2

NILS SCHWERDTNER

Naval Institute Press
ANNAPOLIS, MARYLAND

First published in Great Britain in 2007 by
Seaforth Publishing,
Pen & Sword Books Ltd,
47 Church Street,
Barnsley S70 2AS

Published and distributed in the
United States of America and Canada by the
Naval Institute Press,
291 Wood Road, Annapolis,
Maryland 21402-5034

Library of Congress Control Number: 2008929665

ISBN 978 1 59114 105 1

First published in 2007
as *Die Neuen Queens der Cunard Line*
by Koehlers Verlagsgesellschaft mbh

This edition authorized for sale only in the United States of America,
its territories and possessions, and Canada

Printed and bound in Thailand

HALF TITLE PAGE
**On her first transatlantic crossing the *Queen Victoria* was
accompanied by her fleetmate *Queen Elizabeth 2* – a voyage
that brought about some unique photographic opportunities**

DAVID PIKE

TITLE PAGE
23 February 2006: *QM2* meets her predecessor

CUNARD

CONTENTS

CUNARD! Probably no other name is so thoroughly linked to transatlantic passenger shipping. It may be because the company has always operated top-class ships since 1840. No other concern has produced so many Blue Riband holders. The *Mauretania* speaks for herself, having held the award for twenty-two years, a record. The technical advance which this Cunarder represented cannot express it better. That behind it all was a large fleet of freighters and lesser passenger ships, for which the liners were good publicity, is not so well known.

With the dissimilar sisters *Queen Mary* and *Queen Elizabeth*, Cunard set the standard before the Second World War. The duo dominated transatlantic passenger traffic until the early 1960s, a synonym for British luxury at sea. From the late 1950s the jet aircraft became the new market leader across the Atlantic, signalling the end for transatlantic mass passenger shipping. This made Cunard's decision in the mid-1960s to order a new transatlantic liner, the *Queen Elizabeth 2,* all the more mystifying. Strikebound in the building phase and plagued by technical problems, the ship was eventually commissioned in 1969. Few experts gave this anachronism a chance: that the *QE2* became probably the most successful passenger ship of all time may have been due to the legendary name Cunard. Even if the company had its ups and downs, the ship functioned well, but on one subject the experts were unanimous: she would have no successor as a liner.

When the US Carnival group took over Cunard in 1998 and announced shortly afterwards its intention to build a new transatlantic liner, this was seen initially as a marketing gimmick. The contract was placed, and the ship began to grow at the shipyard. For the second time an alleged anachronism was becoming a reality. As representatives of the Hamburg Cruise Center, when we were first asked if we could turn around the *Queen Mary 2* in Hamburg we were overwhelmed by her dimensions. But Hamburg is a port used to handling the largest container ships in the world, and we were able to say yes quickly.

The preparations for the first visit in 2004 were extraordinarily wide-reaching. When the ship materialised through the morning

INTRODUCTION

mist on 19 July 2004 she was escorted up the Elbe by an armada of boats and small ships. Hundreds of thousands clamoured to see the ship, residents of Hamburg and tourists alike. The streams of visitors exceeded all expectations. There was no rational explanation for the phenomenon. Perhaps it was the enthusiasm in Hamburg for everything British, perhaps the royal name, perhaps simply the size of the ship. Her passengers and crew reacted very positively, and bookings in the aftermath of the first visit expanded enormously.

We were delighted to learn that Cunard had seen the potential of Hamburg as a transatlantic port, and had decided to route the ship to Hamburg twice yearly. Following the first visit, if we were of the opinion that excitement had peaked and we would now have to reckon with fading public interest, we found in 2005 that we were very much mistaken. We were ourselves passengers aboard the ship as she arrived at Hamburg at four in the morning. Even at this hour there were already tens of thousands of people waiting to welcome the ship with a great battery of camera flashes. The turnaround at midday – held back for operational reasons – was the high point of the day, or so many thought, yet better was to come: the midnight departure to a fireworks display. None of those who were present will forget it. No other port ever gave a passenger ship such a reception.

The author Nils Schwerdtner undertook an evaluation of this special ship over a period of forty months. Looking at the career of *QM2*, that seems an appropriate time frame. With a 'one off' ship like this, some faults can occur (as the construction of her predecessor proved; time will tell to what extent the ship will be modified). With his record of work on the first three Queens, Nils Schwerdtner has already proved his technical understanding.

DR STEFAN BEHN
Board member, Hamburg Cruise Center e.V.

FOREWORD

I had the great pleasure of meeting Nils during the course of a transatlantic crossing in August 2006. Nils has an infectious enthusiasm for the sea, great ocean liners and in particular the Cunard Queens.

Cunard is the most famous shipping line in the world. Nils brings to life the great traditions of the company founded by Samuel Cunard in 1840, right through to the modern day, with the retirement of the legendary *Queen Elizabeth 2* and the launch of the splendid *Queen Victoria*.

I commend this book to all those who love the sea and rejoice in the rich history of the Cunard Line.

BERNARD WARNER
Commodore, Cunard Line

CHAPTER

1

THE
QUEENS
OF THE
NORTH
ATLANTIC

'What would Sir Samuel have said?' The American maritime historian John Maxtone-Graham put this question in his 1989 book *Cunard: 150 Glorious Years*, and he meant none other than Sir Samuel Cunard, who in 1840 founded the shipping company with probably the richest tradition in the North Atlantic. In the eyes of his contemporaries this 'small grey-haired man of quiet manners and not overflowing speech' possessed an 'exceptional nerve force and great powers of endurance; [was] brisk of step, brimful of energy and always on the alert' and had the remarkable gift of being able to make 'both men and things bend to his will'.

Samuel Cunard, born on 21 November 1787, was the great-great-grandson of the German

1 June 1936: *Queen Mary* arriving in New York to a welcome from a flotilla of ships, boats and ferries at the conclusion of her maiden crossing

CUNARD

Thones Kunder, who had emigrated in 1683 with his family to the then English Quaker colony of Pennsylvania, and settled in Germantown. Kunder's great-grandson Abraham Cunard was the founder of a successful shipping company, but was deprived of the business after swearing allegiance to Britain in the wake of the American Declaration of Independence in 1776. Abraham Cunard resettled with his family at Halifax, Nova Scotia, part of the British Empire's colony of Canada. Together with the second of his three sons, Samuel, in 1808 he founded A Cunard & Son, a coastal shipping firm which later ran a mail service to Boston, Newfoundland and the Bermudas. When Abraham Cunard retired in 1820, Samuel took over the business, renaming it S Cunard & Co.

**Samuel Cunard
1787–1865**

CUNARD

Thanks to his business prudence and feel for good opportunities, Samuel Cunard built up a fleet of forty sailing ships. He remains to this day one of the most important sons of Halifax. He was a millionaire, a respected businessman and moreover a single parent, raising eight children after the death of his wife Susan in 1823. Cunard, conservative but forward-thinking, became a legend. Although open-minded to useful innovations, he was no pioneer. Cunard left it to his competitors to burn their fingers on new technologies and what he considered audacious business projects. Once he realised that a new concept would be profitable, however, he was the first to go along with it. It is therefore not surprising that in 1829 he replied to a Canadian shipowner who proposed a joint steamship line with him: 'We

are entirely unacquainted with the cost of a steamboat and would not like to embark on a business of which we are quite ignorant. We must, therefore, decline taking part in the one you propose setting up. Your humble servant, Samuel Cunard.'

Cunard's great hour arrived a decade later. Following the first steam-driven Atlantic crossing in 1819 by the *Savannah*, 320 net tons, other shipping firms had followed the example and sent steamers across the 'Great Pond'. *Savannah* was no more than a sailing ship fitted with an auxiliary engine, and only eighty hours of the 663-hour passage was under steam power. Despite the rapid technological advances following the Industrial Revolution, it would be many more decades – in the case of Cunard not until 1893 – before shipping companies dared send their steamers across the Atlantic without auxiliary sails. The age of the steamship began, however, at the latest with the Great Western Steamship Company, whose ship *Great Western* ran something resembling a regular line between Bristol and New York from 1838.

One may assume that Samuel Cunard followed these developments with interest, and in November 1838 he saw his opportunity when the British Admiralty invited tenders for a regular mail-steamship line between Great Britain and North America. Cunard's interest in this venture is clear not least from the fact that in midwinter – the worst time of the year in the North Atlantic – he undertook a voyage by steamship to Britain, sailing in January 1839. Such a passage was never pleasurable. The Atlantic was a dangerous watery waste and one crossed it only if there existed some compelling reason to do so. In its fearsome storms small sailing-ships – and also the first steamers – were the toys of the waves, and all aboard ran the risk of paying for the voyage with their lives.

The subsidy contract which Samuel Cunard was anxious to negotiate with the British government involved the carriage of mail.

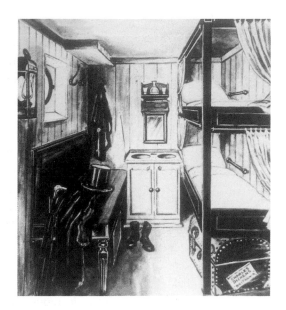

The austere cabin allotted to the author Charles Dickens aboard RMS *Britannia*

CUNARD

Cunard's interest was in freight, and passengers were considered only a secondary source of income. To make the required departure every fourteen days, Cunard calculated that he would need three ships, each of 800 ton gross register, equipped with 300hp engines. In London he arrived quickly at a provisional agreement with the Admiralty, which allowed him to proceed with his shipbuilding plans. The shipping company S Cunard & Co acted as agent for the East India Company at Halifax, and through its head office in London Cunard was recommended to contact the Scottish shipbuilder Robert Napier. An agreement was struck, and Napier set about designing the three ships. Fascinated by the idea of a regular steamship line across the Atlantic, he made his own calculations and made several steamship voyages between Glasgow and Belfast to check his results and understand the requirements better. Finally he convinced Cunard that in order to guarantee reliability, his steamships needed to be larger, and that there should be four. Cunard's finances were exhausted by the original plan for three and so he agreed to enter a joint venture with the Glasgow-domiciled Napier, who then recruited three investors on the local shipping scene – James Donaldson,

George Burns and David MacIver. Together they reconstituted the company as the British and North American Royal Mail Steam Packet Co, of whose £270,000 capital Samuel Cunard held the greatest shareholding of £55,000. Within a short time everybody knew the new company under the name 'Cunard Line'.

In a further round of negotiations with the British Admiralty, conditions were agreed for a ten-year term: the Cunard Line had to offer a fourteen-day transatlantic mail service between Liverpool and Boston via Halifax. Sailings were to be every 4th and 19th of the month, except during the period from November to February, when the winter storms raged and thus the amount of business dropped, and only a single sailing would be necessary each month. For his services Cunard would receive an annual subsidy of £56,000, subject to stringent penalties for the least delay.

The first ship of the Cunard Line was RMS *Britannia*. She was 207 feet long, of 1,135 gross tons and rigged as a three-masted barque. Cabin accommodation was available for 115 passengers, and even though Cunard was anxious to use only the best labour and materials he told Napier to build 'a plain and comfortable boat, not the least unnecessary expense for show'. Therefore the passengers had to settle for a single saloon which served as dining room and lounge and abutted the cabins directly. A cow and some hens were kept aboard to supplement the provisions. Two piston-armed steam engines with an output of 420hp drove the lateral paddle-wheels, twenty-eight feet in diameter, for a top speed of about 9.5 knots.

Britannia sailed on her maiden voyage on 4 July 1840, a historic day for the Cunard Line which is still celebrated today to some extent. Under Captain Henry Woodruff, *Britannia* required twelve days and ten hours for the run to Halifax. She carried sixty-three passengers, among them Samuel Cunard himself and one of his daughters. After a short intermediate stop the ship continued to Boston, where a magnificent reception had been prepared. In recognition of the successful first crossing, the city fathers presented Captain Woodruff with a huge silver trophy, which the company provided henceforth with a place of honour. It can be seen today in a glass showcase aboard *QM2*.

Samuel Cunard was also congratulated for this first success of the new enterprise, and among other things he received 1,873 dinner invitations from the citizens of Boston. During the next six months the three sister ships *Acadia*, *Caledonia* and *Columbia* took their places alongside *Britannia*. The first years were in the main very successful, with a few setbacks. If one reflects on the technical possibilities of those years, and particularly the infancy of marine steam engines, it seems almost a miracle that the Cunard Line not only survived but maintained a service noted for its reliability in spite of the drawbacks. Competition came and went, but during the first decade Cunard was never seriously challenged. Even decades later, when the company was occasionally surpassed by competitors, it always remained in the top rank. While other shipping firms were regularly afflicted by adverse occurrences, the Cunard Line was spared the worst catastrophes. Of course, violent storms exacted their toll in material damage, but to this day the Cunard Line can proudly claim never to have lost a passenger life through the negligence of the company.

Nevertheless, at the outset it had seemed doubtful that Cunard and his partners would be able to celebrate the second anniversary of their creation. After a year it was clear that receipts and the mail subsidy did not cover running costs, and accordingly in September 1841 Samuel Cunard, George Brown and David MacIver showed the Admiralty their ledgers for the first year of operations and requested an increase in the subsidy. On the condition that a fifth ship would be added to

the fleet to guarantee the regularity of sailings, the Admiralty agreed to increase its annual emolument to £81,000 – an indication of their satisfaction with the performance of the Cunard Line.

People on either side of the Atlantic recognised the Line's importance, and this was evident not only from the enthusiastic reception afforded to *Britannia* at the end of her maiden voyage. In the winter of 1843 Boston harbour froze over, and to ensure that the Cunard Line could meet its contractual obligations, volunteers hacked a seven-mile-long channel for passage through the ice. Despite this, Cunard realised that he needed to find another terminal port on the western side of the Atlantic, and from 1847 Cunard ships sailed into New York instead.

If passengers had at first played a subordinate role in his thinking, the rising demand now came to Cunard's attention. Increasing passenger numbers resulted in Cunard's competitors copying his example. These first challenges mostly failed in the face of difficulties after a short period, while the Admiralty subsidy afforded Cunard a clear advantage over his rivals. In 1850 a really serious competitor stepped forward. The American Edward Knight Collins had succeeded in obtaining from the US Congress a subsidy for the creation of a transatlantic mail-steamship line, and like Samuel Cunard he had vast experience in coastal shipping work. The Collins Line ships were larger and faster than Cunard's steamers and offered passengers a modest degree of luxury absent from Cunard vessels. For some years the Collins Line led the field until it was overtaken by disaster. In 1854 the *Arctic* sank after a collision with a French steamship. She went to the bottom with her 322 people, including Collins's wife and two children. Two years later when his *Pacific* disappeared with all aboard – 185 passengers and crew – the fate of the Collins Line was sealed and Cunard

This trophy was awarded to the Cunard Line by the citizens of Boston in recognition of the first successful crossing of the North Atlantic by RMS *Britannia*. The great cup has been admired aboard the company's flagships ever since

AUTHOR

recaptured his leading position.

The time when Cunard could claim to be the undisputed leader was over, however, for European shipping companies were now being founded which would decisively influence North Atlantic services: The Hamburg-Amerikanische Packetfahrt AG (HAPAG, 1856), Norddeutscher Lloyd (1858), Compagnie Générale Transatlantique (1854), Guion Line (1866) and Oceanic Steam Navigation Co (better known as the White Star Line, 1869). The Inman Line had already been founded at Liverpool in 1850. The North Atlantic now became the hardest-fought passenger route in the world. Competition invigorates business, and the effort to lead the field was in the best interests of passenger and freight shipper alike.

At first the German lines were not serious rivals – Cunard operated out of Liverpool and in his estimation the Channel ports had only a minor role – but the British companies fought valiantly among themselves for market leadership. Cunard's motto 'Comfort, Speed and Safety' (the latter attribute in particular being of the essence) helped create for the line an excellent reputation, and thanks to the Admiralty subsidy the undertaking blossomed into a majestic and experienced concern. Cunard's business principle of leaving innovations to others may have proved as much a disadvantage as an advantage, which explains why, in the thirty-year period between 1856 and 1885, Cunard was not among the fastest. That is not to say that the Cunard steamers were poor ships favoured by passengers only for their fine safety record. Samuel Cunard's insistence on using only the best materials and seafaring personnel did not preclude the introduction of all current trends and technical developments. Two things were of special importance to win passengers: speed and comfort, both of which in principle required space, and so within six decades the tonnage rose more than twelvefold from 1,135 gross tons to the 14,281 gross-ton *Saxonia*, which entered service in 1900.

To repeat the original question – what would

Sir Samuel have said had he known that this tonnage would be multiplied by fourteen within another century? In the early years higher speeds meant larger engines and boilers, bigger paddle-wheels and more bunkers for coal. The costs had to be met by more cargo and passengers, to whom the larger steamers offered so much space that in addition to the former saloons a variety of public rooms with names like 'Smoking Room', 'Ladies' Room', 'Writing Room' and 'Library' soon offered the passenger space and amusement. More comfort had to be paid for by the operator, and after a few years a two-class system was introduced with differing degrees of comfort. Catering for the constant streams of emigrants from Europe seeking a better life in the United States, there came the 'tween deck with its dormitories and spartan fittings.

Even if the Cunard Line was not a technological pioneer, wood was replaced in its

Schnelldampfer „Deutschland" (Hamburg Amerika Linie)

At the turn of the century German liner companies seized the initiative in the North Atlantic with such ships as HAPAG's *Deutschland*

AUTHOR'S COLLECTION

ships by iron (*Andes*, 1853), and iron by steel (*Servia*, 1881). Propellers offered many advantages over the sensitive side paddle-wheels (*China*, 1862), and after the introduction of the second screw (*Campania*, 1893), the auxiliary sail was left ashore. The areas of deck formerly needed for sail-handling were replaced by impressive funnels and ever higher superstructures in which the passenger was offered more space (and luxury). Light shafts

were installed to provide the social rooms deep inside the ships with more daylight. Constant developments reformed the machinery, the weak side-pistons being replaced by compound engines (*Batavia*, 1880), which used the steam more efficiently by drawing off the falling pressure using two cylinders – an important step for higher speeds, greater engine efficiency and reduced coal consumption. More efficient boilers with higher steam pressure enabled the steam to be led through another cylinder, and thus the triple-expansion engine (*Campania*, 1893) and shortly afterwards the quadruple-expansion engine (*Ivernia*, 1900) developed from the compound engine. These innovations contributed in stages to increases in speed. While Cunard's first record-holder, *Columbia* of 1841, took ten days and nineteen hours from Liverpool to Halifax at an average speed of 9.78 knots, in 1894 *Lucania* would have won the Blue Riband, had the award existed at the time, with 21.81 knots. For the only slightly longer run from Queenstown, Ireland, to Sandy Hook on the North American coast, *Lucania* needed only five days, seven hours and twenty-three minutes, travelling more than twice as fast as her predecessor. Just as seafaring technology was subject to constant change, the Cunard Line was always abreast of developments.

The last event of significance under the chairmanship of Samuel Cunard was the use of his ships as troop transports in May 1854 after Great Britain entered the Crimean War on the side of Turkey. For his services to Queen and country, Samuel Cunard was knighted by Queen Victoria in 1858. Five years later Sir Samuel retired for health reasons, and he died in 1865. The Cunard Line had good standing, and in order to remain competitive over its North Atlantic rivals became a limited company in 1878 under the title Cunard Steamship Co Ltd.

By now even the German shipping companies were taking a keener interest in the market. The *Elbe* of 1881 was the first express steamer of

A luxury cabin aboard a Cunarder at the turn of the century

CUNARD

Norddeutscher Lloyd (NDL) of Bremen. A total of ten slightly larger sister ships followed, with which NDL operated three departures per week from Bremerhaven. Even if these ships did not match the express steamers of the competition, and lacked their innovations, they still made NDL the largest North Atlantic shipping company in terms of passengers carried. HAPAG's *Augusta Victoria* and her three sister ships could not reach the level of the British from 1889, but closed the gap. Finally it was NDL which in 1897 rang in a decade of German predominance at sea with *Kaiser Wilhelm der Grosse* of 14,349 gross tons. The sleek, four-funnelled 'Great Kaiser' was an exciting ship and her top speed of 22.29 knots won her the Blue Riband in 1898. The competitive spirit also began to grow in the United States, which, since the downfall of the Collins Line in 1858, had played no significant role in mercantile maritime affairs. The banker and industrial magnate John Pierpont Morgan had set out to monopolise transatlantic shipping and so use the shipping lines as an extension of his railway network. After absorbing several smaller shipping companies, in 1902 he set up a trust, the International Mercantile Marine Co (IMMC), which made headlines immediately after its foundation by taking over the White Star Line, one of the five largest operators in the

North Atlantic business and now *de facto* in American hands. Through the business skill of Albert Ballin, Director-General of HAPAG, the German company reached an agreement with IMMC which guaranteed both HAPAG and NDL full sovereignty.

The acquisition of Cunard and the French Compagnie Générale Transatlantique (CGT) would have completed Morgan's plans, but CGT was protected by the French government, and for the British government it was a question of national interest rather than a matter of prestige that Cunard, the last British institution on the North Atlantic, should not end up in American hands. In wartime a strong mercantile fleet for use as troop transports, auxiliary cruisers and supply ships was indispensable, and here Great Britain was being threatened with the loss of its most important ship operator.

To compensate, Cunard was offered substantial funds to resist the recently strengthened German shipowners and the American-run White Star Line with its quartet of very large and comfortable ocean liners. The agreement between Cunard and the British government guaranteed the former a loan for the construction of two record-breakers on the North Atlantic express service. Annual interest on the £2.5 million loan was only 2.75 per cent while the mail subsidy was increased to £150,000 annually, easily enough to cover the interest charge. In return Cunard was required to agree to equip the new ships with certain fittings of military use and to put them at the disposal of the government on request. Cunard was also required to pledge that the company would remain British-owned. As the result of this agreement, in 1907 Cunard commissioned two famous transatlantic liners to end the decade of German domination in the field of speed records. The John Brown & Co shipyard of Clydebank supplied the *Lusitania*, and Swan Hunter & Wigham Richardson of Wallsend, on the Tyne, the *Mauretania*. It was almost taken

CUNARD R·M·S· AQUITANIA

Aquitania **was one of Great Britain's prestigious market leaders before the First World War**

CUNARD

for granted that the new Cunard sister ships would be the largest and fastest ships in the world. Exceeding 30,000 gross tons for the first time, they were 762 feet in length and had a top speed of twenty-four knots, sufficient to complete the Atlantic crossing in five days for the first time. The pair of four-funnelled ships sounded a technological drumbeat for their age: two high-pressure and two low-pressure turbines drove their four screws. Whereas the principle of the steam turbine had been known for some years and was installed aboard warships and coasters, the use in a record-breaker requiring the highest engine output was considered a gamble.

Mauretania and *Lusitania* wrote a new chapter of Cunard history. They did not disappoint in what was expected of them, although they fell short of the luxury offered by HAPAG steamships of the time. Their speed record was convincing although the *Mauretania* in particular vibrated strongly at high speed. The final record was *Mauretania*'s 26.06 knots in 1909 – an achievement which would last twenty years. A third notable ship for the weekly

timetable was *Aquitania*, built by John Brown & Co and delivered to Cunard in 1914. Her speed of twenty-three knots was slower than those of her two partners, but at 45,647 gross tons she was 50 per cent larger. Her increased comfort made her Cunard's first true luxury liner.

All these advances paled into insignificance with the outbreak of war in 1914. While the British blockade forced the German Reich to abandon all foreign trade by sea, the British Empire maintained limited passenger services with those of its ships not required for military purposes. German U-boats, however, made civilian voyages a dangerous business: on 7 May 1915 *Lusitania* was torpedoed without warning and sank. 1,198 people lost their lives.

Contrary to widely held but erroneous belief, the *Lusitania* incident was not the direct cause of the United States entering the war in 1917. After the outbreak of war, *Mauretania* and *Aquitania* were requisitioned with other Cunarders as troop transports. Because of the high British casualty lists in the Dardanelles Campaign, in 1916 they were used as hospital ships before returning to the North Atlantic run in 1917 as transports for American and Canadian troops. A notable victory was achieved by the Cunarder *Carmania*, requisitioned for the role of armed merchant cruiser, when in September 1914, off the Brazilian island of Trinidad, she sank the German raider *Cap Trafalgar* (formerly a passenger steamer of the Hamburg-Süd Line).

During the First World War Cunard lost nine of its fifteen ships to enemy action. After the 1918 Armistice the requisitioned ships were used for some months to repatriate Allied troops before being returned to their owners. Cunard now began the rebuilding of its depleted fleet. The ships which had survived the war underwent extensive renovations, *Mauretania* and *Aquitania* being converted from coal to oil firing. The effect of this was to dispense with the time-consuming and filthy job of loading and

In 1929 Norddeutscher Lloyd's *Bremen* sounded the bell for the last round in the struggle for supremacy in the North Atlantic

AUTHOR'S COLLECTION

trimming coal, while stokers and trimmers were no longer needed for the engine-room. As a replacement for the *Lusitania,* Cunard obtained through the British government the 1913-built former HAPAG liner *Imperator*, the third-largest ship in the world. Renamed *Berengaria*, it joined *Mauretania* and *Aquitania* on the weekly express schedule from Southampton to New York. This enabled Cunard to offer its clientele the fastest and best-balanced service of all North Atlantic shipping companies – closely followed by the

White Star Line, which had a similar but less balanced fleet. For some years Cunard and White Star had the lion's share of this prestigious business, but their French and German competitors were not prepared to leave the field to the British.

The first challenge was made in 1924 by NDL's *Columbus*, a ship of pre-war design which could not match Cunard vessels for speed. The French *Île de France* of 43,153 gross tons, commissioned by CGT in 1927 and as large and fast as the *Aquitania*, was a byword for elegance and good service – a reputation she kept to the end of her thirty-year career. The last round in the struggle for the Blue Riband was initiated two years later by NDL with the 'Ocean Express' sister ships *Bremen* and *Europa*. They were outwardly impressive and internally luxurious, and being 1.5 knots faster than *Mauretania* they regained the Blue Riband for Germany. In 1933 *Europa* lost the distinction to the Italian *Rex*, and the prize passed to the new French record-breaker *Normandie* in 1935.

If Cunard wanted to regain its place against this competition it had to rebuild. Planning for this had begun in 1926. Under the Chairman of the time, Sir Percy Bates, Cunard prepared its return to the top, as at the beginning of the century, with a sensation, declaring it would reduce its weekly timetable on the Southampton–New York run to only two super-liners. It was an audacious step, for it had long been the custom to roster three steamers on the weekly transatlantic schedule, and the planned express steamers would have to meet new demands not only to make themselves economic, but also to defeat the opposition. A weekly transatlantic service with two ships: what that meant was explained by Sir Percy Bates in a letter to Cunard Line shareholders in 1930:

The speed is dictated by the time necessary to perform the journey at all seasons of the year, and in both directions, plus the considerations of the

Sir Percy Bates invented the two-liner transatlantic service and thus indirectly the *Queen Mary* and *Queen Elizabeth*

AUTHOR'S COLLECTION

number of hours required in port on each side of the Atlantic.

The size is dictated by the necessity to make money providing sufficient saleable passenger accommodation to pay for the speed.

In the opinion of its technical advisers, so far from attempting to construct steamers simply to compete with others in size and speed, the Cunard Company is projecting a pair of steamers which though they will be very large and fast, are, in fact, the smallest and slowest which can fulfil properly all the essential economic conditions.

To go beyond these conditions would be extravagant; to fall below them would be incompetent, as the Company would simply be leaving to others a direct invitation to compete with us on more economic terms.

This precise understatement was made to reassure those shareholders who feared that this was nothing more than an outsize prestige project. In fact, Sir Percy's words were not without some foundation: to keep up the weekly sailing intervals, a service speed of 28.5 knots was needed. NDL might just have been able to manage this with its 'Ocean Express' pair, but only on the shorter run between Southampton (not Bremerhaven) and New York, and even then the two German liners would have had no slack for harbour delays or bad weather at sea. Accordingly NDL had completed its team with the modernised *Columbus*.

If only two ships were to carry the same number of passengers as *Mauretania*, *Aquitania* and *Berengaria* had done hitherto, they would actually have to be very big indeed. A ship 1,000 feet long was being spoken of, and only this one ship would be wanted at first; the second would benefit from the experience gained building the first. John Brown & Co of Clydebank was awarded the contract in May 1930, and work began on Order No 534 on 27 December. Cunard kept the name of the new ship a closely guarded secret, and the vessel was

known only by her yard number. No 534 was on the stocks during the Great Depression. Beginning with Black Thursday on the New York Stock Exchange, 24 October 1929, the economies of the New World as well as the Old collapsed in a spiral of falling share prices, bankruptcies and unemployment. Within a few months passenger bookings dropped severely – a development which hit all shipowners in the transatlantic business hard, including Cunard. The darkest day was 11 December 1931, when the Cunard Line's capital had shrunk to the extent that it was barely sufficient to keep the business going. The construction of Yard No 534 was therefore suspended.

It required long-drawn-out negotiations with banks, the shipyard and the British government to master the crisis. No 534 became an affair of state, hotly debated in the House of Lords. Finally the ship's supporters carried the day, not least on account of its symbolic character. If No 534 were completed, it would put new heart into the people. It was agreed that Cunard would receive a £9.5 million loan to build No 534 and her sister ship. This loan came with strings attached, the most important of which stipulated that Cunard would have to merge with the White Star Line (in British hands again since 1927). Thus was Cunard-White Star Ltd dragged out of penury in February 1934, and a few weeks later work resumed on the ship after almost two and a half years.

On 26 September 1934 No 534 was ready for launching, and now the public learned that the new Cunarder would be named *Queen Mary*. The consort of King George V would launch and name the ship after herself. This was a departure from the former nomenclature, in which most Cunard ships were given names ending -*ia*. Presumably the name *Queen Mary* would reflect the fusion with the White Star Line, whose ships' names had traditionally ended in -*ic*. An oft-related story which belongs in legend (but which, much to the dismay of

Work on the *Queen Mary* almost fell victim to the Great Depression

CUNARD

The French flagship was slightly larger, but outwardly the only point of similarity was three funnels – and the *Normandie*'s third funnel was a dummy! The *Normandie* was pleasingly futuristic, the *Queen Mary* rather staid – a contrast continued in the cabins and saloons, where *Normandie* was avant-garde, *Queen Mary* Old English velvet. *Normandie* won the Blue Riband first, but was then exceeded in speed by the *Queen Mary*. *Normandie* recaptured the trophy, but after a few runs *Queen Mary* proved to be the faster of the two.

Work had begun in December 1936 on a dissimilar sister ship to profit from the latest technological developments in construction and machinery. *Queen Elizabeth* was launched at the John Brown & Co yard on 27 September 1938, the name being given by Her Majesty Queen Elizabeth, consort of King George VI. She was Cunard's 'ultimate ship', scheduled to enter service in 1940 to celebrate the Line's hundred-year existence. Only CGT would have been in a position to relegate Cunard to second place with a similar pair of ships, but owing to the war no consort for *Normandie* was ever to appear.

At the outbreak of war, *Normandie* was laid up in New York and in 1942 suffered a major fire caused by workers' negligence during her conversion to a troop transport. *Queen Mary* was New York-bound at the time and lay alongside her French rival after discharging. Meanwhile the incomplete *Queen Elizabeth* was occupying capacity at the shipyard needed urgently for warship construction. That the liner could render useful service as a troop transporter eventually overrode considerations of scrapping the hull for its valuable raw materials. The John Brown & Co yard worked all out to get the ship ready for sea and beyond the range of the Luftwaffe. Under great secrecy *Queen Elizabeth* left the Clyde on 26 February 1940 and, without sea trials, set out a few days later for the United States at high speed. Unreported by enemy or friendly shipping, painted dull

many an aficionado, even appeared in a Cunard publication introducing the *QM2* in 2004) observed that the name *Queen Victoria* had been originally intended for the ship, and that then there occurred a misunderstanding with the Royal Family.

The *Queen Mary* sailed on her maiden voyage on 27 May 1936. High hopes accompanied this well-publicised event, and happily the new Cunard liner did not disappoint despite a few teething troubles. An exciting rivalry now developed between *Queen Mary* and *Normandie*.

Cunard menu cards from the 1960s

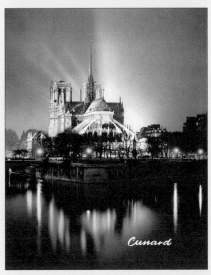

warship-grey and manned only by a skeleton crew, the new liner entered New York on 7 March 1940 and made fast alongside *Queen Mary*.

The 'conscription notices' were not long in coming. Two weeks later *Queen Mary* sailed for Sydney for conversion into a troop transport for 5,500 (her normal passenger capacity being 2,139). *Queen Elizabeth* followed a few months later. Together with *Aquitania*, which had now served in both world wars, and the brand-new second *Mauretania*, the two Cunard flagships worked together in Crown service. During the early war years they were to be found in harbours all around the world, bringing Australian troops to Britain, British troops to the Red Sea and US soldiers to Australia and transporting POWs, all at high speed and in the strictest secrecy. They always managed to give the enemy the slip, if only by a hair's breadth on occasion. As the war went on the Queens were placed under US Navy control and put to the use for which they had been built, to carry large numbers of people across the Atlantic in the shortest possible time – even if the passengers wore battledress.

The Americans designed a 'hot bed' system in which the sleeping berths would be occupied round the clock, making it possible to ship whole divisions. In July 1943 *Queen Mary* set the record with 16,683 crew and troops aboard. By the war's end the two ships had carried 1,242,532 soldiers around the world, causing Sir Percy Bates to estimate that the Cunard liners had shortened the war by a year. After months repatriating Allied troops, both ships were thoroughly overhauled, and not until 1947 did the transatlantic express steamship service designed twenty years previously become reality.

The fifteen years following the Second World War were a last high point in the development of the transatlantic liner. For the last time glamour and splendour would set the tone aboard, the passenger lists were full, and with optimism new tonnage was planned and put into service. The Second World War survivors were joined by the *United States*, which took the Blue Riband from *Queen Mary* in 1952, *Independence* and *Constitution* of the American Export Lines and *Andrea Doria* and *Cristoforo Colombo* of the Italian shipping company Italia. CGT built the last French super-liner *France*

CUNARD QUALITY CRUISES

ATLANTIC ISLES WEST INDIES MEDITERRANEAN

BIG SHIP CRUISING AT ITS BEST

QUEEN MARY MAURETANIA

Following the decline of Atlantic passenger traffic, Cunard took steps to market its vessels as cruise ships

AUTHOR'S COLLECTION

but the Queens remained the great money-spinners on the North Atlantic. The peak was reached in 1957. Never before had so many passengers crossed the Atlantic by ship, and never would they do so again, for 1957 was also the year in which for the first time the number of passengers making the crossing either way by air was equal to the number going by sea. In October 1958 PanAm introduced the first passenger jet aircraft, the Boeing 707, for the North Atlantic service. Where previously the

crossing was a matter of days, now it was hours, and the shipping companies were easily beaten for price. Deep gloom invaded the board-rooms, and the statistics said it all: from 1961 the Queens were loss-makers, losing up to £1 million annually (nowadays fifteen times that). The low point was reached when *Queen Elizabeth* made a winter crossing with only 130 passengers. From February 1963 the two flagships were withdrawn from the regular liner service and used for cruises instead, *Queen Elizabeth* from New York to the Caribbean, *Queen Mary* to southern European waters.

In 1959 Cunard had announced its intention to replace the Queens with a new pair of super-liners. The first of these planned ships, the successor to the *Queen Mary*, was known under the project description Q3. Fortunately the new Chairman of Cunard, Sir John Brocklebank, who took over at the end of 1959, had sufficient foresight to recognise the signs of the times. At first he dedicated himself to a study of the Q3 project, and after intensive negotiations with the British government the necessary credits seemed guaranteed. By now the transatlantic passenger shipping market had begun to collapse. Viewed in retrospect, Sir John therefore made the only correct decision and asked his teams to design a smaller ship with two propellers (the old Queens had four each). It would be possible to retain the same passenger capacity, he reasoned, because the engines would take up less space and an additional deck could be incorporated using materials such as aluminium for the superstructure.

In the course of the commercial development it became ever clearer that the Q4, as the new ship was known, would not be a pure transatlantic liner: although fully equipped technically as a liner, it was also a purpose-built cruise ship, and the three passenger classes that had originally been planned were reduced to two. Ultimately this division was only reflected in cabin and restaurant sizes and furbishings,

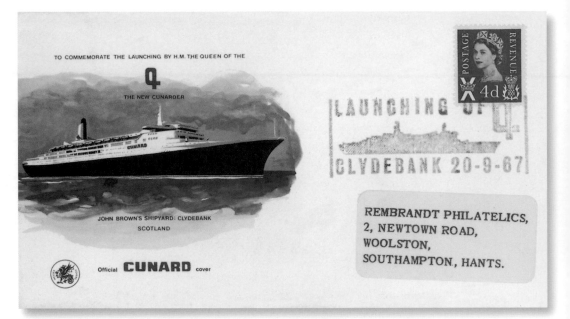

TO COMMEMORATE THE LAUNCHING BY H.M. THE QUEEN OF THE

Q

THE NEW CUNARDER

LAUNCHING OF

CLYDEBANK 20-9-67

JOHN BROWN'S SHIPYARD: CLYDEBANK
SCOTLAND

Official **CUNARD** cover

REMBRANDT PHILATELICS,
2, NEWTOWN ROAD,
WOOLSTON,
SOUTHAMPTON, HANTS.

The name of the new Cunarder was guarded like a state secret. Pre-launch souvenirs bore only the project designation 'Q4'

and all other areas of the ship were open to all. After very difficult negotiations, on 30 December 1964 John Brown & Co received the contract to build Yard No 736. The Q4 was the yard's last major contract for a passenger ship. To finance her construction and reduce the continuing deficits, the Line began to hive off its assets: *Mauretania* left the fleet in 1964, and *Britannic* (last survivor of the old White Star Line) followed in 1965. Two years later *Queen Mary* was decommissioned after a thirty-one-year career. The departure of this revered old liner caused great emotion. However, she was spared the breaker's yard: having been sold to the city of Long Beach, California, she is today at anchor as a floating hotel and museum, a more modest commercial success than in her heyday.

On 20 September 1967 another royal godmother arrived at Clydebank to witness the launch of a new Cunarder. HM Queen Elizabeth II was to name the new ship *Queen Elizabeth* but said: 'I name this ship Queen Elizabeth the Second, may God bless her and all who sail in her.' Why the Queen added the words 'the Second' will probably never be known. Perhaps it was a slip of the tongue. Whatever the reason

it presented Cunard with a problem.

It is important to remember that Queen Elizabeth II reigns over both England and Scotland. Her predecessor, Elizabeth I (1533–1603), was Queen of only England, so that the present monarch is Queen Elizabeth II of England but Queen Elizabeth I of Scotland. To compound the confusion it must be added that Queen Elizabeth (born Elizabeth Bowes-Lyon, 1900–2002) named the Cunarder in 1938 in her capacity as Queen Elizabeth, consort of King George VI, and not as the reigning monarch. The matter of the naming of the new Cunarder was therefore awkward because she had been built in Scotland. To name the ship after an English queen was thus an insult to the Scots. The damage had been done, however, and it would have been a slight to Her Majesty simply to change it back to what had been originally intended. Following discussions with court advisers it was agreed to explain that Her Majesty's intention had been to avoid having two Cunarders both named *Queen Elizabeth*, and this would be reflected by using the arabic numeral '2' instead of the roman 'II' in the name.

In 1968 the first *Queen Elizabeth* and

Cunard's elegant cruise ship *Caronia* took their leave so that finally only two smaller vessels, *Carmania* and *Franconia*, maintained the line service and cruise programme. *Queen Elizabeth 2*, known commonly as *QE2*, was scheduled to enter service the same year but her maiden voyage was postponed owing to delays during construction and then by such a stream of technical problems that Cunard even threatened to refuse acceptance of the vessel. Finally the yard triumphed, and on 2 May 1969 *QE2* was in all respects ready for sea and sailed from Southampton for New York on her inaugural voyage.

No previous break with tradition in the history of Cunard was so palpable as the commissioning of *QE2*. 'Ships have been boring long enough', the publicity proclaimed, and the new flagship was not only outwardly a radical departure from the floating palaces which were associated with Cunard. The streamlined exterior of *QE2* was crowned by a single thin funnel with a wind deflector at its base to keep exhaust gases off the decks. Traditionalists (of whom there are not a few in shipping circles) were appalled to observe that the funnel was

Queen Mary in retirement in sunny California. Less happy was the end of *Seawise University* ex-*Queen Elizabeth*, seen here as a wreck gutted by fire at Hong Kong

AUTHOR'S COLLECTION, CAPTAIN PETER JACKSON

black with a white mantle and that only the wind deflector and company's name on the hull were painted the traditional Cunard red. Even more drastic were the internal modifications: parquet flooring, wood panelling and majestic decoration of the public rooms had all been dispensed with, and instead *QE2* was furnished with what was considered restrained elegance in 1969: glass and stainless steel, dark carpeting, sea-green leather, red tablecloths and Resopal covering for walls and ceilings. Uniformed stewards wearing white gloves and barmen in elegant suits had given way to service personnel wearing the more contemporary roll-neck sweaters. Nevertheless *QE2* received positive acclaim across the board from passengers and

critics alike and her voyages were nearly always sold out. As the remaining passenger traffic across the North Atlantic was now concentrated almost exclusively on the summer months, *QE2* ran the traditional liner service in the summer and cruised in the winter. In order to avoid presenting unnecessary complications for the few passengers who did not travel by air, Cunard and CGT agreed a weekly co-ordinated schedule for the super-liner *France* – at least until the ship was retired in 1974 and left the *QE2* as the only transatlantic liner for the next three decades.

Despite *QE2*'s success, Cunard did not return to profitability. The beginning of the 1970s confronted Cunard with new difficulties: drastic rises in fuel prices and high wage claims from

7 May 1969:
***QE2* was afforded a great reception upon her arrival in New York following her first North Atlantic crossing**

STEFAN BEHN COLLECTION

union-organised crews, especially on the two older ships *Carmania* and *Franconia*, and the weak structure of the undertaking itself put Cunard's future in doubt. This changed in 1971 when Trafalgar House Investments Ltd, a 10 per cent shareholder in Cunard, bought the company for £27.3 million. There followed a radical and painful restructuring process whose only objective was to make Cunard profitable again and establish it on the market as an elegant cruise-ship organisation, all as an independent sector of Trafalgar House. *Carmania* and *Franconia* and their British crews were cut adrift. From Overseas National Airways, a 100 per cent Cunard-owned subsidiary, the company took over two cruise ships being built in the

America 1972

There by QE2.
Two weeks in America plus a cruise to Bermuda on the new Cunard Adventurer.
Back by BOAC.
All from £294.

NEW! AMERICA 7 HOLIDAY

YOU CAN BOOK ALL THESE HOLIDAYS AT
COOKS
8 PUMP STREET
WORCESTER WR1 2QU
Tel: WORCESTER 28229

In the early 1970s Cunard attempted to enter the modern cruise-ship market with sister ships *Cunard Adventurer* and *Cunard Ambassador*

STEFAN BEHN COLLECTION

Netherlands, which entered service respectively in 1972 as *Cunard Adventurer* and *Cunard Ambassador*. Registering these vessels under flags of convenience meant savings for the company in taxes and other disbursements as well as crew

salaries. At the same time the still-young *QE2* received her first face-lift, in which her restaurants were enlarged so that all passengers could dine at a single sitting. Furthermore, a block of luxury suites with balconies was installed on a part of the Sports Deck between the mast and funnel. The two new acquisitions had only brief careers with Cunard. Although the idea was not wrong in principle, the ships, at 14,150 gross tons, were thought small and exclusive and proved rather restrictive in operation. *Cunard Ambassador* was badly damaged by fire in 1974 and sold to a Danish operator for use as a cattle transport. *Cunard Adventurer* was also sold off two years later.

To replace them Cunard took possession of two other cruise ships on the stocks, which entered service in 1976 as *Cunard Countess* and *Cunard Princess*. The two sister ships had been ordered by the film company MGM, which wanted a fleet of eight tourist cruise liners to complement its movie work. Once these plans were abandoned Cunard added the four-star ships to expand its own fleet, but in spite of serving for two decades they never really succeeded in forging their own identity, nor did they find much of a place in the Cunard story, nor were they even a perceptible presence among the cruise ships of their time. This may have been linked to the fact that, as with their predecessors *Cunard Adventurer* and *Cunard Ambassador*, Cunard had not been involved in the original design. The ship plans had been worked out by an undertaking which had no experience in the building and business of cruise ships. *Cunard Princess* and her sister had 'paper-thin walls', a plus point for a TV soap opera but certainly not for luxury cruise ships. Whereas Cunard Line's position as a cruise-ship operator was secure in the business politics of Trafalgar House, that was not enough to provide the former transatlantic organisation with a new identity, nor to found a new approach by innovation. In 1983 Cunard bought Norwegian

American Cruises, which was in dire financial straits, and so acquired its popular luxury cruise ships *Vistafjord* and *Sagafjord*. To retain the clientele the ships were left under the Norwegian flag, their names unchanged and the Norwegian crews retained. The five-star ships also retained their luxurious interiors, with which Norwegian companies had made their name in the cruise-ship market. In 1986 the extremely luxurious cruise ships *Sea Goddess I* and *II* were added to the Cunard fleet when the company bought up the Norwegian company Sea Goddess Cruises. These 340-foot-long cruise yachts, each with accommodation for only 116 selected passengers, elevated Cunard from the mass market to the British, American and Norwegian luxury class. What that signified for the future development of the company will be examined in more detail in the next chapter. This introduction must now mention two important events in the career of the *QE2*.

On 2 April 1982 Argentine troops occupied the Falkland Islands (population 1,813) and the South Georgian Dependency. No resistance was offered. The Falklands lie about 400 miles off the Argentine coast, and at 8,000 miles' distance from the British Isles the colony is the furthest remaining outpost of the formerly gigantic British Empire. At the time of the invasion

TOP
Franconia and her sister ship *Carmania* were the last ships of the 'old' Cunard fleet when the *QE2* entered service

AUTHOR'S COLLECTION

MIDDLE
The Lookout Bar with a view over the forecastle was sacrificed when enlarging the kitchens during *QE2*'s first major refit.

STEFAN BEHN COLLECTION

BOTTOM
Cunard served the mass market into the mid-1990s with the sister ships *Cunard Princess* and *Cunard Countess*

CUNARD, STEFAN BEHN COLLECTION

Argentina was under a military dictatorship led by General Leopoldo Galtieri. The country had serious economic and political problems. In this situation Galtieri acted as other statesmen before him had done in times of crisis and attempted to divert attention from his problems at home by a political success offshore. The Falklands had been wrangled over for years. The military *junta* considered that Great Britain would not take military steps to retrieve the situation and probably imagined that only diplomatic sanctions would be applied. For the British

Prime Minister, Margaret Thatcher, the invasion offered the opportunity not only to improve her political image (British success in the Falklands Conflict contributed largely to her re-election in 1983) but to show the world that the former empire still maintained a place in the circle of the superpowers. Thus the Falklands Conflict became a mixture of conflict in deadly earnest, with fighting and losses suffered by both sides, and a piece of overseas political theatre.

As in both world wars, merchant vessels were required in a supporting role for the conveyance of naval and land forces. Within a few days the first troops had boarded the North Sea ferry *Norland* and the P&O liner *Canberra*. The *QE2* was 'conscripted' on 3 May 1982 on finishing a transatlantic crossing. While passengers were still disembarking by one gangway, workers were already boarding by another to convert the liner into the biggest troop transport of our times. Eight days were allowed for the work. On 12 May the 5th Infantry Brigade, made up of the 1st Battalion Welsh Guards, 2nd Battalion Scots Guards and 1st Battalion, 7th Duke of Edinburgh's Own Gurkha Rifles, came aboard. By the use of field beds the capacity of *QE2* (normal passenger capacity at this time, 1,870) was raised to 3,150 men. The ship had 640 crew, all of them volunteers.

All movable luxury objects – furniture, plants, works of art, several hundred pound of caviar and 17,000 bottles of sparkling wine – were shipped ashore, the carpets were covered over with wooden panels, the Double Room was converted into a mess hall, and charts of the

TOP
In 1983 Cunard acquired the Norwegian luxury cruise ships *Vistafjord* and *Sagafjord* from Norwegian American Cruises

AUTHOR'S COLLECTION

BOTTOM
In 1986 Cunard added the luxury yachts *Sea Goddess I* and *II* to its fleet

CUNARD, STEFAN BEHN COLLECTION

QE2 menu card motif for Valentine's Day, 1978

STEFAN BEHN COLLECTION

occupied during waking hours with distance running around the ship and in weapons training, helicopter exercises and simulated emergency evacuations of the ship; even in their free time there was no let-up. On the night prior to arrival the bridge officers had the sternest test of an otherwise uneventful voyage: thick fog lay over the sea and *QE2* had to cross a major ice field. Contrary to his instructions, but in agreement with the military commanders aboard, Captain Peter Jackson had the radar turned on briefly every half hour. *QE2* arrived intact in the roadstead at South Georgia on 27 May 1982 and anchored, disembarking troops and supplies next morning.

In view of her status as a national icon, it was decided not to send the ship into the immediate war area around the Falklands. After forty-eight hours, with only sixty tons of supplies remaining aboard, the unloading was halted on the threat of Argentine air attacks and *QE2* set off for home with 640 survivors from the sunken warships *Antelope*, *Coventry* and *Ardent*. Home waters were reached on 11 June 1982. *QE2* was the first ship to return home from the war zone, and her welcome was therefore a warm one. Off the Isle of Wight the liner was met by the Royal Yacht *Britannia* carrying HM the Queen Mother, who signalled her thanks to the returning servicemen.

After 14,967 miles of active service *QE2* was released to Cunard by a grateful government. In the opinion of Captain Jackson, the Falklands campaign was the best thing that could have happened to the *QE2*. In previous years the liner had received sharp criticism. A reduction in service standards and the quality of the food had been accompanied by disparaging remarks about the furnishings, which had once been much admired. What might have been *chic* in 1969 had now been surpassed. Government funds for a complete refit of *QE2* following the Falklands Conflict came just when they were needed. It had taken just eight days to convert the luxury

Falkland Islands were hung on the staircases in place of the carefully chosen portraits. Parts of the aluminium-framed windows enclosing the aft sun deck were removed to create a landing platform for Sea King helicopters. Another helicopter deck was installed on the forecastle. A pipeline ran through the Deck 2 access door down six decks of stairway to the fuel tanks for refuelling *QE2* at sea. Armament was a fixed machine gun on each bridge wing. Weapons, materials, kit and provisions were loaded aboard.

The voyage to South Georgia lasted fifteen days, during which time the men were kept liner into a troop transport, but the reconditioning work would take nine weeks. Under normal economic conditions this would be an unthinkable and intolerably expensive lay-up, but Cunard had been well compensated for the military employment of its flagship.

In August 1982 *QE2* resumed her regular transatlantic and cruise schedules, her hull painted light grey, her funnel Cunard red, and a variety of her public rooms modernised. The hull livery was not liked, and the classic black replaced it after a few months, but the red funnel with two black bands remained, much to the approval of passengers, crew and traditionalists. Finally it was agreed that *QE2* looked like a pure Cunarder. At about the same time a large contingent of the British service staff was replaced by Filipino stewards, whose work was generally considered more satisfactory. While the home labour force complained at the toil in this sector and submitted regularly spaced demands for better pay, the Cunard Line found

From 1983, *QE2* reappeared as a true Cunarder in the traditional livery of black hull and red funnel

STEFAN BEHN COLLECTION

After the Falklands Conflict, *QE2* continued with her hull painted pebble grey for several months

STEFAN BEHN COLLECTION

it could make major savings by employing Filipino staff. This was a setback for British employees but proved better for passengers in that by their own standards the Filipinos received excellent remuneration – and money is an important motivating factor in the workplace. Thus it comes as no surprise that the service sector aboard today's cruise ships worldwide is in Filipino hands.

The affection and recognition accorded to *QE2* for her role in the Falklands campaign were turned to good use and Cunard ensured that its flagship had her regular overhauls at the

Winter 1986–7: one of the new diesel engines being lowered through the funnel opening

MAN B&W DIESEL AG

scheduled times. This was decisive in the second important event for the *QE2* in the 1980s.

Although as a rule she was usually booked to capacity, the *QE2* was an expensive ship to run. Throughout her career, her engines had been prone to breakdown. They consumed 600 tons of fuel oil daily in an era of steadily increasing crude oil prices, and the Cunard board now assessed whether it would be more beneficial to give the ageing ship a comprehensive overhaul – fitting her with new engines – or make a greater investment in a new flagship. They decided on a general refit on the grounds of her familiarity to the public and lower cost. Accordingly, on 27 October 1986 the eighteen-year-old-steamship entered Lloyd Werft at Bremerhaven to be converted to a motor vessel. The German concern had won the contract to renovate her and replace the old steam turbines with modern diesels.

QE2 spent 179 days at Bremerhaven. Her engine-room was systematically gutted, and her boilers and turbines replaced by two AEI-built electric motors. Their working current would be produced henceforth by nine MAN B&W diesels coupled to generators. Social rooms and cabins were modernised, and *QE2* received an additional block of prefabricated luxury suites, these being installed between the existing suites

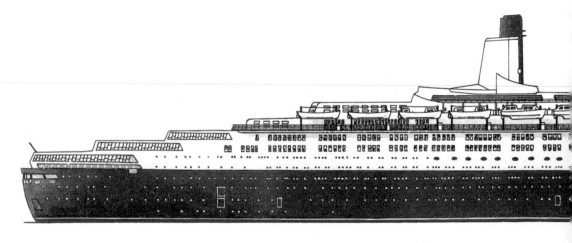

and the funnel. The silhouette of many classic liners suffers by such changes, but in the case of *QE2* her admirers were almost unanimous that her appearance had improved over the years: not least in the current refit by having a bolder funnel to balance the additions to the upper structure. The new motors equipped *QE2* for the twenty-first century, it was claimed. That this major refit lasted her for more than another twenty years at sea shows how rewarding this investment proved for Cunard. At the time of her re-entering service nobody could predict what radical events were to confront the line in this epoch.

The Cunard fleet in 1985

CUNARD

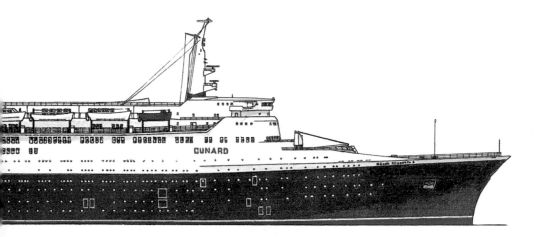

QE2 drawn by Dietmar Borchert to 1:1000 scale

2

**Impressive publicity:
the famous Cunard red and black funnels**

CUNARD, AUTHOR'S COLLECTION

CUNARD MAKEOVER

1990 marked 150 years since the first voyage of RMS *Britannia*, and Cunard celebrated this anniversary with theme voyages and other special events throughout the year. The flagship *QE2* had moored at Yokohama on 28 December 1989 under charter for six months as a floating hotel and exhibition centre to the promoters of 'World Exposition 1990'. After a few Pacific cruises *QE2* returned to New York on 7 July 1990, and her subsequent voyages that year matched the theme of her owners' 150th anniversary. Under Captain Robin Woodall she had made her fastest transatlantic passage to date, leaving New York on 17 July and arriving at Southampton four days, six hours and fifty-seven minutes later for an average speed of 30.16 knots. Next the liner became the star of a special kind of birthday celebration for Cunard when, fully booked, she departed from Southampton for a gala voyage around the British Isles, her first stop being at Cobh, where the ship's arrival inaugurated the new container terminal. For thousands of Irish emigrés, Cobh – formerly Queenstown – had been the gateway to the New World. Not a few of them had sailed aboard Cunard steamers. This was the first visit of *QE2* to the port, and 60,000 spectators turned out to see the historic liner. Although the *QE2* attracted customarily large crowds of sightseers at ports of call around the world, it was the visit to Liverpool the next day that passengers and crew would long remember. Half a million people crowded the banks of the Mersey for miles as the *QE2* entered the city where the Cunard story began. Although the old Queens bore the port of registry 'Liverpool' at the stern, none had ever gone there. Even though registered at rival Southampton, *QE2* was received by Merseysiders as an honoured guest.

At Greenock, at the seaward end of the Firth of Clyde, close to the place where *QE2* had

been built and run her trials in its waters in 1968, a visit to the former John Brown & Co shipyard was not now possible: *QE2* was the last great liner to have been built there, and since the closure of the yard the river had sanded up and no longer had the depth to take a big ship. Instead, retired shipyard workers were given the chance to make a nostalgic visit to the ship. The call at Cherbourg was an anti-climax but rates a mention since it was here that the ship's Master, Captain Robin Woodall, relinquished command to his relief captain, Ronald W Warwick, in order to exercise his role as the ship's representative during the later part of the gala voyage. Captain Warwick thus became the first and to date only ship's master in Cunard history to have commanded the same ship as his father: *QE2* had made her maiden voyage under Commodore William E Warwick. The high point of the festivities was a special Fleet review

QE2 began a new chapter in her career in 1987 with new engines and a bolder funnel

FOTOFLITE

in the Solent to celebrate the Cunard anniversary. The Line was represented by *QE2*, *Vistafjord* and the container ship *Atlantic Conveyor* of the Cunard subsidiary Container Line. A number of smaller ships took part, and as guests of honour the Queen and Prince Philip were present aboard the Royal Yacht *Britannia*, escorted by the Trinity House vessel *Patricia* and the frigate HMS *Broadsword*. At midday the royal party transferred to the *QE2* by launch to dine with Captain Woodall and the Trafalgar House Chairman, Nigel Broakes. Her Majesty was on the bridge as *QE2* berthed later at Southampton. The anniversary was rounded off by the 500th crossing of the Atlantic by *QE2*, the 'Cunard ports' of the first days being revisited with a cruise from New York to Boston and Halifax in September.

A 150th anniversary is an opportunity for reflection and taking stock. As was mentioned in

Crown Dynasty (pictured), *Crown Monarch* and *Crown Jewel* joined the Cunard fleet through a joint venture with the Crown Cruise Line.

CUNARD, AUTHOR'S COLLECTION

Chapter 1, *QE2* was the last ship designed and built specially for the Cunard Line. The remainder of the fleet consisted of ships acquired from other companies. The former Chairman of Cunard, Ralph Bahna, stated of the purchases of *Sea Goddess I* and *II* in 1986:

With this acquisition, Cunard will be the world's only cruise operator offering three completely

different types of luxury from which to choose, ranging from the superliner *QE2* to the highly personalised *Sagafjord* and *Vistafjord*, to the private yacht-like cruising of the *Sea Goddesses*. The addition of the Sea Goddesses into the Cunard family will help solidify Cunard's pre-eminence at the top end of the luxury cruise market.

Noteworthy in this statement is the omission of the *Cunard Countess* and *Cunard Princess* as a fourth category of luxury: even if the sister ships were used exclusively for one- and two-week luxury cruises for the American mass market, ships rated four-star should really be considered luxurious. The statement underlined the board's firm belief that success was to be achieved by trying to appeal to a very broad variety of travellers – or, less flatteringly, that Britain's former ships of preference in the North Atlantic had become a mixed bag.

Cunard Princess and *Countess* served the American general tourist market; the two *Sea Goddesses* were at the other end of the spectrum, being ultra-luxurious yachts for the very rich, who would meet their own kind aboard: between them was a luxury segment represented by the *Sagafjord* and *Vistafjord*, with which Cunard competed against innovative Norwegian shipping companies with exquisite service, and finally *QE2*, a ship of her own unique class, was a British icon in the tradition of transatlantic passages. So at which sector of the public was Cunard aiming? In view of its increasingly hazy position, the question was raised even during the 150th anniversary celebrations, and expert reporters were already beginning to recognise the company's increasing lack of direction. While other operators targeted definite groups and mass-tailored their tonnage accordingly, Cunard no longer seemed to have a clear clientele. It was not outstanding in any single area. Since its takeover by Trafalgar House, the Line had relied on its history and was venerated by everybody

who treasured the traditional British image. This played an increasingly important role in the wave of nostalgia which began in the 1980s and persists to this day, but whereas it might be the case with *QE2*, it did not apply to the whole Cunard fleet.

Thus during the 1990s various business ideas evolved, none of which came to anything or provided a clear line to follow. In 1990 Cunard had talks with the American Shipbuilding Company of Tampa, Florida, regarding the building of two cruise ships for the American market. Presumably the two vessels, with 900 to 1,200 beds, would have replaced the only moderately successful *Cunard Countess* and *Cunard Princess*, but the idea remained unfulfilled. Next the concept of a new transatlantic liner which Cunard referred to as the 'New Queen' was taken to the market research stage. Only a few years before a new ship of this type had been ruled out in favour of new engines for the *QE2*, but now apparently a new ship for the basic Cunard route might be ruled in. Whether Q5, as the technical press

called it, could have been a success must be doubted. Cunard had a *de facto* monopoly of North Atlantic passenger transport by sea and thus could estimate the likely demand. The potential builder would be a Japanese yard to keep costs down. The style would match the elegance of the *Queen Mary*. Cunard was not only going to its roots but also building on the prevailing nostalgic trend.

A questionnaire circulated to former passengers to evaluate the possible prospects for such a project spoke of a ship able to complete the crossing in three and a half days, thus challenging all past records for the Blue Riband. The material was candid enough to admit that Cunard's intention with the 'New Queen' was to compete with the airlines. In view of the passage price, rated at $2,175, how were the costs to maintain the required service speed of thirty-five knots to be financed?

The only passenger liner ever to have made a passage so fast was the *United States* – and this ship had been decommissioned in 1969, not least for her high fuel consumption. While the

'New Queen' would make transatlantic crossings mainly in summer and cruise in winter, the *QE2* would concentrate on the cruise market and back up the North Atlantic service in the high season. The 'New Queen' was abandoned at the conceptual stage, and then unexpectedly the *United States* came into focus instead. This had as its origin a joint venture between Cunard and the Crown Cruise Line, a subsidiary of the tourist conglomerate Effjohn International.

Under the name Cunard Crown, Cunard brought in *Cunard Princess* and *Cunard Countess* while Crown supplied the *Crown Monarch* of 15,000 gross tons, commissioned in 1990, and the brand-new sister ships *Crown Jewel* and *Crown Dynasty* of 19,000 gross tons to round off the fleet of the joint venture. Marketed as comfortable ships for the middle classes, each was used for 'adventure cruises' in different sea areas. The demarcation line between the Cunard

Crown ships and the luxury cruise ships of the Cunard Line was not clearly drawn. For Cunard, the construction of new cruise ships was now set aside. The joint venture, although originally agreed for ten years, was of short duration. *Crown Monarch* returned to the house flag of her original owners in 1994, and in the course of Cunard's internal revamping, explained later, the charters for *Crown Jewel* and *Crown Dynasty* were revoked in 1995 and 1997 respectively, so that the Cunard Crown partnership faded into obscurity.

This short time span is typical of the business politics of Cunard in those years, and is noteworthy only for the entry of the liner *United States* into the picture. The largest passenger vessel ever built in the United States had deprived the *Queen Mary* of the Blue Riband with apparent ease. It must not be forgotten, however, that the *United States* had been heavily

Vistafjord was among the vessels assembled to celebrate the fiftieth anniversary of D-Day

CUNARD, AUTHOR'S COLLECTION

subsidised by the US government as a potential troop transport (remembering the two Queens in the Second World War). In 1969 the United States Lines had ceased operating its last passenger ship and turned to cargo. The low passenger count on the North Atlantic run, high running costs and continual labour unrest among the crews justified the decision to shut down the operation. Attempts by a Seattle operator in the 1980s to recommission the *United States* as a cruise ship failed for lack of finance, and in 1992 the undertaking went into liquidation. In the subsequent auction of the ship, Fred A Mayer, Chairman of Commodore Cruise Lines, and the Turkish shipyard owner Kahraman Sadikoglu bid the highest price of $2.6 million and obtained her for Marmara Marine Inc, an associate firm in Delaware. Like Crown Cruise, Commodore Cruise was a subsidiary of Effjohn International, and while the *United States* was in the Mediterranean for asbestos stripping, Mayer arranged a deal between Effjohn and Cunard under which Cunard would operate the renovated *United States*. Even transatlantic crossings in tandem with the *QE2* were mooted. The conversion work on the *United States* fell through in the end because of financial difficulties. The disembowelled liner returned to the USA in 1996 and was laid up at Philadelphia. In 2003 the vessel was obtained by Norwegian Cruise Line for the purposes of modernisation, but she remains moored alongside a pier near Philadelphia's Walt Whitman Bridge at the time of writing with no apparent progress on the planned restoration.

The first half of the 1990s was therefore an active period for Cunard, although no clear line was being followed which would make the future direction of the company visible. After Cunard celebrated its 150th anniversary in great style, in 1994 *QE2* marked her own twenty-fifth birthday with a programme of events. Before passing to these, the flagship merits a closer look.

In common with her owners, *QE2* lacked a little uniformity. To keep its flagship abreast of the times, over the years Cunard had invested millions in modernisation work, both aesthetic and technical. In the early 1990s, however, the ship had begun to look her age. The plastic ceiling panels of 1969 were replaced by the decor of the early 1980s, and ten years later she had furniture and textiles corresponding to the tastes of the early 1990s. Thus the *QE2* offered elegance, but the overall impression was of a mixed bag of styles. Nevertheless, even in the 1990s *QE2* was one of the most successful ships in the worldwide cruise trade. On her transatlantic crossings she was always well booked. As a cruise ship she was equally convincing and her annual world voyage, as a rule between January and April, was almost legendary. Undoubtedly the *QE2* had matured during her career, and not only had faithful fans and a loyal clientele but attracted positive opinions both from passengers and the technical press. The liner had long since emerged from the phase of ailing service at the outset of the 1980s. Her special status among the passenger ships of the world ensured that she was never out of the headlines for long, and since people like sensation, even the most minor occurrence was found worthy of a mention in the newspapers.

QE2 provided good reason for excited headlines in 1992. On 3 August she should have sailed from New York for the Bahamas, for seasoned cruise passengers an unspectacular programme. The Bermudian authorities, however, refused to issue the necessary landing certificates because the islands had reached their maximum tourist quotas. At short notice Cunard substituted a voyage with visits to Bar Harbour resort, Newfoundland and Halifax. The last stage of the cruise was the island of Martha's Vineyard off the coast of Massachusetts – the holiday resort of the rich and famous. The ship was under the command of Captain Robin Woodall on the evening of 7 August when she

weighed anchor. It was a clear evening with a light breeze. The pilot, John F Hadley, was on the bridge to assist in navigating the shallow and rocky waters of the Vineyard Sound before the liner headed back to New York. At 2158 crew and passengers felt a sudden vibration followed by a violent jolt. The crew showed no alarm, but on the bridge for a moment there was perplexity. Captain Woodall brought the ship to a stop. The engine room reported that all was well. There had been no collision. Only after the Chief Officer had made a damage control check and sounded the tanks in the ship's bottom was it reported that the *QE2* had grounded. For the pilot and ship's officers this was a shock, since the depth and state of the tide should have provided adequate clearance for the draught of the ship, some thirty-two feet. A survey showed that two freshwater tanks, a ballast tank and an empty fuel tank in the double bottom had flooded with seawater.

Shortly after the grounding the Staff Captain announced to the passengers the reason for the jolt, adding that no water had entered the ship's interior and there was no danger. Later that night a US Coastguard ship arrived and, aided by a *QE2* tender, checked for oil spillage. An oil slick surrounded the ship, but was proved to have come from the damaged empty tank. The passengers were landed next day at Newport by *QE2* boats and three ferries, after which the liner proceeded under her own power at slow speed to Boston to dry-dock. At the moment of contact, *QE2* had been making twenty-five knots, and this high speed, together with the ship's great mass, had resulted in considerable damage,

the extent of which was now to be seen. The keel was damaged over a length of some 300 feet. There was a seventy-five-foot-long gash to the bottom starboard side, but the damage extended for half the ship's length and a number of steel plates had been depressed by up to fourteen inches. She had come out of it well, however: many a modern cruise ship whose thinner plating would not have been designed for the vagaries of the North Atlantic winter might not have got off so lightly.

QE2 was given temporary repairs at the Boston yard, but as the shipbuilding industry in this region of the United States had gone into decline over the years and lacked qualified workers, a full repair was not possible. Cunard offered the job to yards in the United States and Europe, and awarded it to Blohm + Voss at Hamburg. This was convenient insofar as *QE2* was booked there for a winter refit to exchange one of her engines. Unfortunately these new engines were not yet available, and she left Hamburg on 4 October only to return to the Elbe at the end of November. Yard charges, loss of income from seven cancelled voyages and compensation to passengers cost Cunard £30 million. And ironically this had come about because the liner had not been able to enter Bermuda as planned.

A year later, on two very stormy transatlantic crossings, *QE2* demonstrated that she was still the same and that the yard had done its work well. In September 1993 she endured a Force 9 storm with seas of between twenty-three and thirty feet in height. The worst of these hit her broadside-on and threw the ship over 19 degrees to starboard. When she was struck again a few hours later, the inclination was 21 degrees. About fifty passengers were thrown down, and some required treatment in the ship's hospital, while numerous items of porcelain were smashed and a piano wrecked. On a westwards crossing in December 1993 she inclined over 22 degrees during a Force 10 hurricane with seas up to fifty feet in height, forcing Captain Keith Stanley to reduce speed to thirteen knots. Numerous shipboard activities were cancelled and those passengers wanting to dine found bare tables in the restaurants, on which cutlery would be set only on request. Once the storm abated, Captain Stanley resumed at 32.5 knots, the maximum speed possible, in an attempt to make up for lost time, but even so *QE2* arrived ten hours late in New York. As she was scheduled to sail the same day on a Christmas cruise to the West Indies the turnaround – the time needed for cleaning the ship, refuelling, disembarkation and embarkation between voyages – was cut to three and a half hours, which earned *QE2* an entry in the *Guinness Book of Records*.

The renovation of *QE2* at the end of 1994 involved the relaying of 409,000 square feet of carpet, work on 861,000 square feet of fabric and the installation of 3,329 new chairs and 1,805 tables

In May 1994 *QE2* had been in service for twenty-five years. By coincidence, a few weeks before she had exceeded 3 million sea miles sailed – more than the *Queen Mary* and *Queen Elizabeth* combined. The anniversary was celebrated on 11 May at Southampton with a commemorative lunch for invited guests, and following the tradition set by the 150th anniversary celebrations, the liner made a special cruise in British waters, visiting Greenock and Liverpool among other places. In June 1994 *QE2* participated in a ceremony celebrating the fiftieth anniversary of D-Day, an event in which her illustrious forebears had been involved. Recalling the great armada which had assembled in June 1944 for the Normandy landings, a fleet of twenty-seven ships of all kinds gathered off Fort Gilkicker near Portsmouth for review by the Royal Yacht *Britannia*. Besides the *QE2* were also present the P&O cruise ship *Canberra*, Southampton's museum ship *Shieldall*, Cunard's *Vistafjord*, the cruise ships *Black Prince*, *Kristina Regina*, *Statendam*, *Crystal Harmony*, *Silver Cloud* and *Seabourn Pride*, the Victory ship *Jeremiah O'Brien* and the US aircraft carrier *George*

Washington. After the review on 4 June, the fleet arrived next morning on the French coast to remember the Allied victory. On board *Britannia* were members of the Royal Family, HM the Queen, HRH the Duke of Edinburgh, HM the Queen Mother and HRH the Princess of Wales, together with numerous VIPs and leading politicians including the British Prime Minister, John Major, and President Bill Clinton of the USA. A fireworks display on the coast at Le Havre rounded off the spectacular event, in which a total of eighty ships of various nations had taken part.

While *QE2* carried out her normal programme of cruises and North Atlantic crossings during the second half of 1994, Cunard was arranging for its 'Grand Old Lady', as the liner had become known, to undergo a twenty-fifth-birthday face-lift to rid the ship of the mixed decors aboard. A figure of $45 million was being discussed – a lot when one remembers that only seven years previously Cunard had invested a considerable amount in modernisation of the ship. However, whereas the aim in 1987 had been to give the ship twenty more years technically, the new idea was that she should be appealing visually, too. As no British shipyard had the necessary resources, three German concerns were the leading competitors for the three-week renovation contract: HDW of Kiel, Lloyd Werft of Bremerhaven and Blohm + Voss of Hamburg. The last won the order. In the official jargon of the company, the work was to involve the renovation of 963 cabins and their bathrooms and to rearrange the public rooms to provide the ship with a uniform, harmonious design and to improve its passenger flow.

The 1990 anniversary had shown how much interest remained in the historical era of ocean voyages a quarter century after the eclipse of the North Atlantic passenger lines – whether from potential passengers who had experienced these times and for whom the *QE2* was the last opportunity to wallow in nostalgia, or from younger people who had missed the period and wanted the chance to experience a pure Atlantic crossing. Whereas Cunard had turned away from its past in 1969 with the phrase 'ships have been boring long enough', there now occurred a rethink in which the *QE2* was advertised as the last representative of a magnificent past, and the Line's historical aspect was thrust deliberately to the forefront. Accordingly contractors received orders to refurbish the public rooms – MET Studio Ltd and John McNeece Ltd were asked to give the *QE2* a decor that would be timeless yet would also awaken in passengers memories of 'the good old days'. During the summer of 1994, sections of the cabin areas were sealed off from the rest of the ship for renovation work and to be searched for remnants of asbestos.

The major work began on 13 November 1994 when *QE2* sailed from New York for Hamburg direct, with workers but no passengers aboard, arriving at her destination seven days later. A few

days before, the German press had reported on the important order for Blohm + Voss, and so despite the grey winter weather several thousand Hamburg people gathered at the dockside to welcome the ship. Some preliminary work had already been done at sea, and so 2,500 fitters, tinsmiths, electricians, upholsterers and other tradesmen began working round the clock for the next three weeks to give *QE2* her face-lift. Only 550 of these were Blohm + Voss personnel, the remainder being subcontractors hired either by the shipyard or by Cunard directly. Outwardly the classic black hull livery was replaced by the colour 'Cunard Steel Blue', a dark shade of navy blue which from a distance could be mistaken for black. No less than sixteen tons of paint was needed for the change.

A red, gold and blue stripe along the upper deck was not to everybody's liking since to some it appeared to resemble a 'rally stripe'. The Cunard lion above the ship's name in red on the upper hull was better received, but both the lion

Between 1994 and 1999 *QE2* had a navy blue hull and a gold, red and blue stripe along her superstructure

KAI ORTEL

and the rally stripe disappeared during renovation work five years later. In the interior the basic layout was retained, but most rooms were refurbished, receiving a sort of 'neo-art deco' look, while some favoured areas were enlarged. The designers had intended originally to expand the Midships Lobby on Deck 2, which served as an access area for passengers, into an atrium two decks high incorporating the Purser's Office: the upper level would have had a

One of the window displays on the Heritage Trail inaugurated in 1994

AUTHOR

surrounding balcony, and one can assume that an elegant staircase was to have connected the two levels. In the end the room retained its original form. The trumpet-shaped Formica columns alone survived from 1969. The sixties-style ceiling with its concentric circles was given a visually quieter look, and the four sofas at the edge of the sunken floor were retained. In place of the former chromed rails behind it, wood-panelled balustrades were fitted. To make the Midships Lobby a real adornment it was given four murals by Peter Sutton telling the story of the Cunard Line in a kind of collage. Two decks up, on the Quarter-Deck, the Magrodrome, the glass sliding roof over one of the pools which had been installed only eleven years previously, was removed and replaced by a solid deck. The pool itself was also removed to convert the

former Club Lido into the Lido Restaurant: equipped with its own kitchen and bar and having no fixed seating order, it offered a simple alternative to the restaurants. The removal of the Magrodrome created additional space on the deck above, and by removing a stairway and the toilets the popular Yacht Club Bar could be enlarged extensively fore and aft to become the Yacht Club, an elegant night club with room for a band and dance floor. The former Mauretania Restaurant on the Upper Deck moved down a deck to make way for the Caronia Restaurant for first-class passengers (insofar as one could speak of two classes of passenger aboard *QE2*, except in relation to choice of restaurant and cabin size). With its green tones and cool art deco style and partitions of frosted glass, this dining room paid homage to Cunard's 'green goddess', the *Caronia* of 1947. For this reason the horse theme of that popular luxury cruise ship was taken up and given impressive emphasis by an illuminated sculpture in aluminium by the artist Althea Wynne. The area in front of the restaurant was used for the new Crystal Bar, which would serve passengers in the Caronia Restaurant and the Princess and Britannia Grills with drinks before dinner, reflecting the green theme of the restaurant.

The Theatre Bar on the Upper Deck was replaced by the rustic Golden Lion Pub, which took its name from the lion in the Cunard crest. Designed to imitate an English hostelry, it would encourage lively evening discussions and serve quality beer. The former Midships Bar was replaced by the Chart Room in maritime decor, with a prominent illuminated chart of the North Atlantic behind the bar serving area and a grand piano from the *Queen Mary* in a corner. The Grand Lounge was reconstructed with a new stage and dance floor, new sofas being added in a different arrangement. It was intended overall that the promenade corridors near the public rooms would be widened for easier passage. In the case of the Queens Room, for example, this meant that the promenade areas would be chair-free. As the space between the promenades was restricted, sliding panels were installed to partition areas off as required. Finally Cunard introduced a novelty for connoisseurs: the Heritage Trail through the entire passenger area, making the *QE2* a floating museum with authentic exhibition pieces from Cunard's 155-year history. Pride of place among the ship models was given to an authentic builder's model of the 1907 *Mauretania*. Some sixteen feet long, with long rows of illuminated portholes, it stood in a glass case in the foyer of the Mauretania Restaurant. Elsewhere in glass showcases were fine arrangements of cutlery, models, publicity material, a *Queen Mary* lifebelt and the silver trophy awarded to Captain Woodruff of *Britannia* in 1840 by the Bostonians, which is now displayed aboard *Queen Mary 2*. Additional

In 1996 and 1998, *QE2* was a guest at Hamburg

RUDOLF GRIMME

eye-catchers hung in all stairways were the original oil paintings portraying historical or modern Cunarders, and portraits of the British Royal Family. With the liner thus fitted out, the transatlantic passage of the *QE2* was to have been a triumph as she showed off her new finery.

QE2 left Dock 11 at Blohm + Voss as planned on the night of 13 December 1994 and headed down the Elbe for Southampton. The yard could pride itself on having completed the refit

to time despite an extremely tight schedule. Not so the subcontractors hired by Cunard. Even as *QE2* was under way, workers were still finishing cabins, modernising bathrooms and making the public rooms presentable. A two-day voyage to show off the conversion work and familiarise the crew had to be cancelled. In view of the amount of refurbishment work still to be done, the British Board of Trade issued a certificate reducing the passenger capacity from 1,760 to 1,000, this figure including more than 300 workers remaining aboard for the transatlantic voyage, whose task was to have the ship ready in time for the two-week Caribbean cruise following her arrival in New York.

Most of the passengers who had booked but been denied places were advised in time, but 190 could not be contacted and arrived at Southampton with their luggage only to be turned away. Some 600 to 700 'lucky' passengers were now to endure between 17 and 22 December 1994 what the press called 'The Christmas Hell-Voyage of the *QE2*'. Preceding the arrival of the ship in Manhattan were horror stories about the appalling conditions aboard, flooded cabins, unfinished public rooms, stinking water in the swimming pool and a brown brew coming from the water taps. To make things worse, a Force 8 to 9 gale had given the *QE2* an uncomfortable crossing which not only hampered the work but laid low a number of workers with seasickness.

John Olsen, Chairman of Cunard, came aboard off the American coast with the sea pilot to be received by a passengers' sit-in. He offered a full refund of the fare and a free voyage with Cunard as compensation. What sounded like a generous offer did not find acceptance with all passengers and, in a joint action led by an attorney who had been a passenger on the 'hell-voyage', they sued the Line for $100 million. A year later agreement was reached whereby each passenger received $5,000 compensation, and an extra $2,000 was given to those who had been on the following Caribbean cruise, during which the shipboard work was finally completed. John Olsen bore the brunt of the blame. The company had made an operating loss of £6.9 million in the second half of 1994, and he was paid off with a 'golden handshake' of £232,000 to be replaced by Peter Ward, a former director at Rolls-Royce. This incident would probably have been much worse for Cunard had QE2 not been well booked ahead. Even if many passengers on the coming world voyage had

> **Cunard Line**
>
> ## Queen Elizabeth 2
>
> Trans Atlantic Voyage
> No. 1014
>
> *Westbound from Southampton and Cherbourg
> to New York City.*
> *7th September – 12th September, 1995.*
>
> Record of contact with
>
> ### *Hurricane Luis*
>
> on
> 10th and 11th September, 1995.
>
> The following information was
> recorded in the ship's log:
>
> *Highest winds – 130 miles per hour.*
> *Average wave height – 40 feet*
> with one specific wave at 0205 hrs (11 Sep) estimated at 90 feet.
> *Nearest position to the "eye" – 130 miles.*
> *Ship's speed reduced to 5 knots.*
>
> *Captain R. W. Warwick*

A Passenger Certificate from the *QE2* commemorating the voyage through Hurricane Luis

CUNARD, STEFAN BEHN COLLECTION

gone aboard mindful of the bad press, the new interior design spoke for itself. Thus the waves of indignation gave way to words of the highest praise, and 1995 turned into one of the best years ever for Cunard. In June that year another anniversary was celebrated – the ship's 1,000th voyage. And if anybody still doubted the fact, she provided the proof herself that a cherished and well-cared for liner does not belong on the scrap-heap at the age of twenty-five.

Under the command of Captain Ronald Warwick, QE2 left Southampton for New York on 7 September 1995. The meteorological report had promised an uncomfortable crossing because Hurricane Luis had moved towards

Newfoundland, whipping up the North Atlantic to fury. Since Luis was turning to the north-east, Captain Warwick decided to steer a south-westerly course to avoid the hurricane's path. On the night of 10 September, however, 140 miles from the eye of the storm, QE2 encountered wind speeds of between fifty and a hundred knots, and seas between thirty-three and forty feet high. In the early hours of the morning Captain Warwick hove-to to wait until the storm abated – a wise decision, for at 0210 a monster sea ninety feet high was sighted. He reported later:

> The sea seemed to take an eternity to reach us, but it was probably not even a minute before it broke over the bow of QE2 with tremendous force. An enormous jolt ran through the ship followed by two smaller jolts a few seconds later. At the same time the sea swamped the whole forecastle including the bridge, and it was several seconds before the water drained from the windows of the wheelhouse and one could see out again.

Warwick told the press that the sea had looked like the cliffs of Dover rolling towards him in the night. There were no injuries aboard. Next day the passengers received a commemorative certificate of the incident, and feeling took hold that QE2 was a fantastic ship in which one could feel safe and protected in the most difficult sea conditions. The ship herself did not get off scot-free. The forecastle rail was bent and some of the decking at the forepeak had been ripped outwards.

While QE2 had proved herself once more and shown that she was good as new – indeed finer – there began to crystallise in the thinking at board level the idea that the time had come to change direction and shed some of the fleet. In future, Cunard would concentrate exclusively on the luxury sector of the cruise market: Cunard would become the world's great luxury-ship operator. With this in mind, in June 1994 *Royal Viking Sun* was acquired from the Royal Viking Line,

Royal Viking Sun with Cunard red funnel and Royal Viking logo

CUNARD, STEFAN BEHN COLLECTION

which had gone into liquidation. The ship, first in service in 1988, had an excellent reputation and outstanding assessments but seemed to lack character. Together with *Vistafjord*, *Sagafjord* and the two *Sea Goddesses* she was now marketed under the new banner Cunard Royal Viking. As with the two older ships, the Norwegian crew and Scandinavian atmosphere so popular with passengers were retained.

Cunard's new direction signalled a retreat from the mass market. As we have already seen, the charter business with the three Crown ships had had only a short existence, and Cunard's *Princess* and *Countess* were also up for sale. *Cunard Princess* left the fleet at the beginning of 1995 to join the Mediterranean Shipping Company (MSC), and eighteen months later *Cunard Countess* went to the Awani Cruise Line. While it was the board's purpose to embark upon a return to tradition, showing the flag in the increasingly competitive cruise market, the mother company Trafalgar House, which had 34,000 employees in construction, engineering and the energy market, and had profited considerably from the British economic liberalism of the 1980s, had run into troubled waters. The devaluation of sterling on the international money markets and the concurrent recession in its main branches had forced Trafalgar House into the red during the first half

of the decade. Its shareholders found the takeover offer of the Norwegian Kvaerner concern for the sum of £904 million attractive, and on 4 March 1996 it was accepted unconditionally.

Kvaerner had been founded as a shipyard at Oslo in 1853, but had quickly extended its activities into the energy market and paper production. It had grown steadily, and besides the production of oil and gas, oil rig construction and shipbuilding (at the time of the takeover Kvaerner owned twenty-seven shipyards), building and engineering featured among its core activities. At the beginning of the 1990s Kvaerner had begun a phase of accelerated expansion. The purchase of the British competitor seemed a favourable step towards becoming a concern of global importance. Whereas shipbuilding was among the traditional interests of the Norwegian company, and Kvaerner's shipyard empire had significant standing, the Managing Director, Erik Tonseth, made no secret of the fact that running a cruise-ship company did not feature in his plans and that in due course Cunard would be sold off.

The cruise-ship market therefore expected that Cunard would soon pass into new hands, the only question being to whom and under what conditions. Cunard's mixed bag was not an attractive proposition for operators of modern and homogenous vessels. Of its competitors, only P&O made known immediately after the Kvaerner takeover that it was interested in Cunard, but only on its own terms. A quick sale was not Tonseth's way of doing business, and since Cunard was a shipping company in upheaval he was in no hurry to dispose of it hastily and possibly at less than its market worth. Therefore Kvaerner held on to it to provide the opportunity for its regeneration. The market knew that Cunard really needed a massive infusion of cash for profitability and to regain its status at least in the eyes of the traditionalists: the question was whether Kvaerner was prepared to do that.

A comparison of the *QE2*'s
stern in 1969 and 1999
shows the modifications
over the period

STEFAN BEHN COLLECTION,
CUNARD

A series of minor and greater occurrences in which Cunard was involved in the course of the ensuing months may not have been seen as encouraging by the new Norwegian owners. The year 1996 was to be the last season with Cunard for the thirty-one-year-old *Sagafjord*, since she was now considered past her best: she needed a major overhaul in order to be suitable for the new direction in the luxury market. Her final year with Cunard was ended abruptly by a fire in her engine-room on 26 February 1996. Nobody was hurt and the accommodation area was undamaged, but repair was considered not worthwhile and *Sagafjord* was decommissioned.

A few months later new life was breathed into the ship. When the American firm Regency Cruise Line went bankrupt, it caused the German tour operator Transocean a problem. Transocean had wanted to charter from Regency its cruise ship *Regent Sea*, better known to enthusiasts as the former Swedish transatlantic liner *Gripsholm*. *Regent Sea* was now arrested in port, and for Transocean the laid-up *Sagafjord*

was the quick solution to the problem. She was about the same size as *Regent Sea* and was dry-docked at Singapore at short notice for repairs. Sporting new funnel insignia but still easily recognisable as *Sagafjord*, the chartered Cunarder embarked upon her new career as *Gripsholm* on 15 July 1996. She had bad luck, however. Only three weeks later while on voyage from Copenhagen to Kiel she grounded at Öresund, the narrows between Sweden and Denmark, and went into Lloyd Werft for repairs to propellers and hull.

On 4 April 1996 *Royal Viking Sun* sustained hull and engine damage on a coral reef in the Red Sea. Preparations made to evacuate the passengers were cancelled once it was ascertained that the ship was in no danger. She was towed to Sharm El-Sheikh and held in lien at anchor by the Egyptian government until Cunard paid $23.5 million compensation for damage to the protected reef. Afterwards *Royal Viking Sun* went into a yard at Malta, where a further half a million pounds were paid out for repairs to the hull. The ironies of fate here are that after the collapse of the Regency Cruise Line, the passengers who had booked a world cruise on the *Regent Sea* were transferred to the *Sagafjord*, and after her engine-room fire her passengers were shipped aboard *QE2* or *Royal Viking Sun*, both also sailing world cruises: and when the *Royal Viking Sun* grounded at the end of her voyage she had some of the original *Regent Sea* passengers in her cabins. *Sagafjord* had only been recommissioned because of the cancelled *Regent Sea* charter. While the *Sagafjord* charter was to run for five years, it was cancelled after only six months when Cunard sold the ship to the British tour operator Saga Holidays, an organisation whose target group is the over-fifties. Renovated at great expense, *Sagafjord* began her third career under the name *Saga Rose*.

A rather curious incident occurred on a *QE2* voyage from Cadiz to Lisbon when, after a slight jolt was felt during the passage, it was discovered at Lisbon that the ship had 'harpooned' a whale. A crane was needed to remove the fifteen-ton animal. Since whales usually give ships a wide berth, it was assumed that this specimen had already been dead at the time of the collision.

The next Cunarder to earn a negative headline was the *Vistafjord*. In 1997 she suffered three shipboard fires. In February a cupboard in the crew area caught fire, causing negligible damage. In April a short circuit caused a fire in the passenger laundry. The material damage was kept in bounds but a steward died of smoke inhalation during the attempt to extinguish the fire. While *Vistafjord* was undergoing a refit at Malta in May 1997, fire broke out in the crew laundry. One voyage had to be cancelled. The passengers were reimbursed and received in addition vouchers to the value of $1,000 each.

This series of accidents was certainly no incentive for Kvaerner to persevere with Cunard, but nevertheless the Vice-Chairman, Antti Pankakowski, stated in March 1997 that a partner for the *QE2* was under consideration. Though it

greeted the news with interest, the press guessed that the project would only come to fruition once Cunard completed its current phase of restructuring and returned to profitability. Five months later it became known that negotiations were proceeding between Kvaerner and the Vlasov group of Monaco for the sale of the Cunard Line. Vlasov was acting as intermediary and would later become the ship manager. The real buyer was not named, but it was said that the intention was to build three new luxury cruise ships, each to carry 600 passengers. An asking price of about $400 million was rumoured, at the rate of exchange then in force about a third of what Kvaerner had paid for Trafalgar House. It was precisely this poker play for the best price to hive off the former Trafalgar House companies that led ultimately to the downfall of the Kvaerner empire.

1998 was a black year for the Norwegian industrial giant. The board was forced to admit that it had exceeded itself in the purchase of Trafalgar House. Besides the astronomical price of £904 million ($1.2 billion), it had also inherited a mountain of the British conglomerate's debt. The 1997 Asian crisis toppled Kvaerner into the red, and by the end of 1998 the concern had debts of around $12 billion. Not surprisingly, plans to expand Cunard fell through in a radical shake-up of the industrial giant. What its board had hoped to avoid was now happening on the grand scale: the 'necessary putting down' of all subsidiaries not part of the core business, and this did not stop at the shipbuilders, upon whom Kvaerner had grown big and who were now loss-makers.

Cunard was spared this fate. At the last moment the company was saved, and what JP Morgan and IMMC had failed to do a hundred years before now became reality: the Cunard Line, for many an ultra-British institution, fell into North American hands. In the light of the impending Kvaerner sell-off it was probably the best thing that could have happened to Cunard.

C H A P T E R

3

ATLANTIC DAWN

On 3 April 1998 there occurred another turning-point in the long history of the Cunard Line when the British company was transferred into US hands. Under the chairmanship of the founder's son, Micky Arison, the Carnival Corporation obtained 68 per cent of Cunard's shares so that the concern was now effectively controlled by Carnival's US cruise-ship empire. The remaining 32 per cent was acquired by Carnival a year later. The takeover received a mixed response from the technical world and enthusiasts: clever negotiations had resulted in the final sell-off of a British cultural inheritance. Ship lovers now envisaged an Americanised Cunard Line in which cutbacks in crew numbers (and passenger comfort) would be thought fitting for the new Internet age. Realists were of the opinion, however, that money and experience were wanted to provide Cunard with the new face which the company so urgently needed, and they realised that neither Kvaerner nor Cunard itself

had been able to fulfil this requirement, though Carnival could. The experts even perceived a dual strategy on the part of Arison. They thought that Kvaerner's initial retention of a minority shareholding in Cunard could be a pathway into shipbuilding. Order books at cruise shipyards worldwide were full, some with long waiting lists due to the tourist boom. Carnival itself had several ships under construction or in waiting with Kvaerner. It could not be foreseen then that Kvaerner's dire financial circumstances would result soon afterwards in the abandonment of its shipbuilding interests and the transfer of its remaining shareholding to Carnival. On the second decisive point in the Cunard takeover by Carnival, Arison had allowed himself to be persuaded by his business partner, Atle Brynestad, founder of the Seabourn Cruise Line in 1987, with two yachts for especially luxurious 'premium cruises'. Seabourn was 50 per cent owned by Carnival, and Brynestad had suggested to Arison that they buy up Cunard and use the company's long history to build up its identity. A modernised Cunard Line aiming at the luxury sector fitted perfectly into the Carnival portfolio, closing the gap between the mass market (Costa Cruises and the Carnival Cruise Lines) and the expensive Seabourn Yachts business. At the same time it prevented a rival from buying Cunard and competing with Carnival's Holland America Line.

The restructuring began at once, and the path suggested by the Kvaerner management, to turn Cunard into a company specialising in meeting passenger demands for high quality, was now pursued. First a corporate identity had to be created – a face for the firm so unmistakable that even the non-expert would know at first glance 'That is Cunard'. As a first step Cunard was merged with Seabourn Cruise Line to become Cunard Line Ltd, thus giving the two undertakings a common marketing platform. *Royal Viking Sun* and the two *Sea Goddesses* were more suited to the Seabourn clientele and after

their transfer were renamed *Seabourn Sun*, *Seabourn Goddess I* and *Seabourn Goddess II*. Thus within only three years the Cunard fleet had been reduced from eight to only two ships, *QE2* and *Vistafjord*. Soon afterwards came the announcement that in future Cunard would be targeting the British market so as not to impinge on Carnival's Holland America Line. For this purpose *Vistafjord* underwent an expensive renovation, was re-registered at Southampton (instead of the Bahamas), and was given the classic Cunard name *Caronia*. After sixteen years she had at last renounced her Norwegian roots to suit the new Cunard image. When she left Lloyd Werft at Bremerhaven in December 1999 even her ardent admirers had to admit that the ship had been improved by the conversion work. She left the yard in the classic Cunard livery of black hull, white upper works and red funnel.

Caronia had been built originally for the Norwegian America Line for seasonal use as a transatlantic liner (although she had never been used as such). She had the liner's elegant silhouette and in her new livery she looked the part. For the *QE2*, already closely matching the image of the new Cunard Line, an extended 'beauty treatment' was announced for the end of 1999. Although this was only a superficial renovation, the new Cunard owners came up with a minor sensation two months later. Micky Arison recalled: 'This was around the time of the *Titanic* movie. We were all talking about this overwhelming nostalgia movement in the country. What if we built the next great ocean liner?'

On 8 June 1998 the new Cunard director Larry Pimentel announced that the Cunard Line would be building a new liner for the transatlantic service. Before a meeting of Norwegian shareholders in Oslo he revealed 'Project Queen Mary' to the public for the first time. In his address he said:

The project will lead to the development of the

A selection of Cunard brochures over the years

(CUNARD, AUTHOR'S COLLECTION)

grandest and largest liner ever built – the epitome of elegance, style and grace. It is our objective to build a new generation of ocean liner that will be the very pinnacle of the shipbuilder's art; the realisation of a dream of another time. Our goal is nothing less than to create a new Golden Age of sea travel for those who have missed the first.

On the basis of these grandiose words a questionnaire was circulated to various shipyards. Responses came from across the board with designs for seasonal cruise ships, but these did not correspond to the ideas of Arison and Pimentel. It had become clear that the design for a transatlantic liner meant in many respects a new beginning, and Arison entrusted the task to the thirty-eight-year-old in-house naval architect of Carnival Corporation, Stephen Payne. Payne's interest in passenger ships had begun in 1967 after he saw a report on the original *Queen Elizabeth* in a British TV programme for children, *Blue Peter*. After the ship was gutted by fire at Hong Kong in 1972, the then twelve-year-old wrote a letter to the BBC, predicting that in the future another ship of this size would be built. This was improbable in 1972 and it was even less likely that the author of the letter would be the man to design the first pure-bred ocean liner in three decades.

A passenger ship is not simply a passenger ship, and despite the modern merging of the terms there are substantial differences between a cruise ship and a ship for line service (hence the word 'liner'). These differences arise primarily from the operational requirements: cruise ships usually operate in fine-weather zones in order to provide their guests with a pleasant holiday experience. Accordingly they do not need to be built as extreme-weather ships, for as a rule adverse weather can be forecast so far in advance that it can be avoided. This means that a relatively light construction method will be sufficient. The ship's draught will not exceed twenty feet, so that even small and remote

harbours of shallow depth can be visited, and a great saving in fuel will be obtained as against ships of greater draught.

While cruise ships are mostly of shallow draught, the trend over the years has been to create as much marketable space above the waterline as possible. In place of terrace-like sun decks, most modern passenger ships have a towering superstructure, a short forecastle and a steep, cut-off stern. As in a block of flats, every square foot of surface space on the ship is used. While this pays off in relatively calm waters, this kind of silhouette with great windage – and shallow draught – may prejudice safety and passenger comfort in rough conditions.

As regards the transatlantic liner, the Atlantic in summer may sometimes resemble a duck pond, but mariners know it as a stormy and dangerous ocean. To ensure that a ship on these routes can keep to a tight schedule, she must have certain qualities. A reinforced hull will enable a liner to withstand a hurricane without sustaining structural damage. The weighty plating necessary for this purpose will give the ship more draught (the *QE2* for example has 32.5 feet) and better sea-keeping qualities in heavy seas. A long forecastle looks elegant but its primary function is to intercept heavy rolling seas and divert them to protect the superstructure against damage. Long, terrace-like after-decks give the liner a relatively low silhouette with less wind resistance. Speed is important for a liner. A cruise ship wanders around dreamy tropical islands at a relaxed pace, but on the North Atlantic run in the past a fast crossing was the most important thing, and some of that urgency persists to the present day. Moreover, a liner requires enough reserve oil bunkers to wait out a storm and then try to make up for lost time. Greater speed means more output and more powerful engines, and this in turn increases fuel consumption: 'Having been given the chance of designing the new Cunard transatlantic liner in May 1998, initially

As Chairman of Carnival Corporation, Micky Arison provided the incentive to build *QM2*

CARNIVAL CORPORATION

codenamed Project Queen Mary', Stephen Payne recalled later, 'I wondered what would be the best way to tackle the task. After some thought I decided that a review of *Queen Elizabeth 2* would be a good starting point.'

'Stephen, in your lifetime, you will only have one opportunity to design such a ship,' Micky Arison told his chief architect, 'so you had better get it right the first time! After this ship, I don't quite know what I am going to give you to follow on. Nothing will ever compare with this.' Payne came quickly to the conclusion that Cunard needed a full-blooded ocean liner, not a cruise ship that looked like a liner.

In the final analysis a liner is considerably more expensive to build and run than the equivalent-sized cruise ship. I argued from the outset that if the transatlantic route was to be maintained then a liner would be required and not a cruise ship. I feared that if a faux liner was built and was run on a short transatlantic season in August, popularity would dictate the ship being operated between July and September, then June to October and May to November, and that within this sort of time frame the ship would statistically soon encounter a typical North Atlantic storm and come off second best with her reputation tarnished.

necessary fuel and reserve tanks had to be engineered in. These two factors would lead to higher running costs and would have to be balanced out by the installation of a huge number of cabins, as many as possible of them with an expensive balcony. The final consideration was the construction material for the superstructure. Aluminium had been used extensively on the *QE2* upper decks to provide an extra deck with no increase in draught. Since Payne was working on a thirty-year lifespan for the ship (Cunard eventually agreed on forty years with the builder), aluminium was out of the question. Although it is lighter than steel there are difficulties in working aluminium and steel together, while the lighter metal tends to become brittle with age, as fissures and rips in certain areas of the *QE2* upper works have shown.

Payne preferred an all steel ship. This would mean that 'Project Queen Mary' would have one deck fewer than *QE2* if the same dimensions and draught were retained, but for the number of passengers required to make the liner profitable, much more space would be needed to carry heavy steel upper works and thus a larger hull and more powerful engine plant.

As a result of these considerations the ship quickly expanded from the original estimate of 85,000 gross tons, and very soon it was evident that Cunard had embarked upon a project to build the world's biggest-ever passenger ship with no equal in length, beam or height. The actual dimensions were limited only by the size of the turning basin at Southampton and the height of the Verrazano Narrows Bridge at New York. Two years passed before the planning phase was completed except for individual minor problems. A team investigated the ports that *QE2* had visited in her career to ascertain whether the new ship would be able to enter them. Besides the technical decisions in Payne's design, the practical and aesthetic also played a role. For Payne it was important

Payne thus persuaded Arison to authorise the planning for the first North Atlantic liner since the *QE2*. That she served as the example was obvious, but in the thirty years since the construction of Cunard's former flagship, shipbuilding had made such strides that 'Project Queen Mary' had to be developed from first principles. For the foregoing reasons the new ship could not be built in the typical box form. More valuable, marketable space in the upper structure would be sacrificed for a long forecastle and extensive after-deck, while machinery for a service speed of 28.5 knots (as against the twenty to twenty-four knots of a cruise ship) and the

that the new ship bore a close resemblance to the *QE2,* and thus he included numerous classical elements of style, provided always that they had some practical purpose, as for example the wave-deflector on the foredeck, which was similar to the fitting on the French line's *Normandie* of 1935.

That the *QE2* as originally designed was to have been a three-class ship put into service as a single-class one can be seen today from her deck plans. Despite all modifications, the arrangement into sections remains confusing. Here Payne saw the need for improvement. One deficiency of the *QE2* was the lack of a continuous exterior promenade. Although it is possible to go around the superstructure forward in fine weather, a stairway has to be negotiated which is often closed for strong winds on the North Atlantic run. Payne found his inspiration to solve this problem in the 1959-built

Rotterdam, where the forward part of the promenade deck is shielded by glass windows. His compromise, combining safety with utility in a manner pleasing to the eye, may not be to the taste of all traditionalists, but is successful. Ships such as the *QE2* and *Maxim Gorky* ex-*Hamburg* of the same era, or the 1929-built *Bremen,* were not hailed as beautiful by all their contemporaries because innovations broke with ocean-liner tradition, but nevertheless they became design icons.

Stephen Payne's design impresses by its sheer size (one may well imagine that in their day ships such as the *Queen Mary* evoked similar emotions), but it also shows the further logical development of the classic transatlantic liner, whose growth has been stunted hitherto by cruise ships and the decades-long break in the art. Abaft the long forecastle with its rising bow and the wave-deflector stand the majestic upper

The first *Queen Mary* had a rounded bridge front with free-standing bridge wings. The shape and colour of the *QM2*'s bridge face are a tribute to the earlier vessel

ANDREW KILK. THORBEN KOCKS

Between *QM2*'s nautical rounded edges are long rows of balconies, a concession to the expectations of today's passengers

CUNARD

works. For both practical and aesthetic reasons Payne decided to build the bridge face to emulate the first *Queen Mary* with her stepped, continuous half-round decks. To reduce the surface exposed to possible monster waves, Payne smoothed the form into a convex shape crowned by the massive all-glass bridge. Recalling the original *Queen Mary*'s free-standing bridge wings, and to detract somewhat from the massive impression of this facing, broad black stripes adorn the side wings of the bridge front. On the rear side of these side wings port and starboard, protected from the weather, are installed panoramic lifts, which provide a superior wind-protected view over the ocean.

Deck 7 is the uppermost deck within the hull itself (the so-called Shelter Deck). Above it the superstructure is set inboard from the ship's sides far enough to create space for a broad Promenade Deck to encircle the ship, terminating astern in one of the sun decks, and forward in a kind of tunnel with panoramic windows behind the bridge face. The sun decks at the after end of the structure are stepped and offer plenty of space for sunbathing and free-time activities. Between the sun decks and bridge face, mainly visible in side profile, are the concessions to market necessity: midships from the Promenade Deck upwards, Payne's creation with its rows of balconies looks like a block of holiday apartments afloat. Since most passengers nowadays demand this kind of luxury, no sympathy could be expected for the sensitivities of maritime historians.

Stephen Payne succeeded in blending this ugly element harmoniously into the whole. Moreover the economics of 'Project Queen Mary' required a further two decks of cabins with balconies. To ensure that ship stability was not compromised by these additions, Payne installed three further decks of cabins with balconies in the upper hull, the balconies having the character of a gallery of large apertures cut into the hull. The ship is crowned by a single

funnel of unmistakable similarity to that of *QE2*, but more squat to allow passage below the Verrazano Narrows Bridge, and thus more robust-looking. While the project was still in the initial drawing-board-and-computer stage, the technical world and ship fans waited impatiently for information on size, equipment, building yard, commissioning date of the ship and her name. Even if the project name was *Queen Mary*, enthusiasts thought a historic Cunard name possible. *Britannia* was the favourite, after the first Cunard steamship. The thinking behind this was that the Royal Yacht was to be decommissioned in 1997 and the public wave of emotion would favour a new ship of that name.

Though Cunard was flooded with enquiries for more details, few were released, mainly because of the intricacies of the design of such a unique ship. By the end of 1999 Payne and his team had progressed sufficiently for Larry Pimentel in Miami to release basic information and a computer sketch:

Ever since we announced we would build a giant classic liner, our mail has been flooded with requests for information and wherever I go I am besieged by questions about her. Guests have even sent in deposits without knowing the specifics of the product or the deployment. Candidly, they want to be the first guests on the first ocean liner to be built in three decades. While we realise that details of this wonderful project are eagerly awaited, we are proceeding prudently and deliberately. The grand scope and cost of the project dictates this approach. We can't be, and we won't be, rushed.

Meanwhile, invitations to tender for the contract had been distributed to five European shipyards: HDW of Kiel, Meyer Werft of Papenberg, Kvaerner Masa of Turku, Finland, Harland & Wolff of Belfast and Alstom – Chantiers de l'Atlantique, St-Nazaire. After comparing technical completion dates, time schedules and

An aerial photo of the shipyard at St-Nazaire, showing the cruise ships far left *R-One*: white ship astern of her *Seven Seas Mariner*, right margin *Infinity*, in rectangular pool above, *Mistral*

economic factors this number was quickly reduced to two. At the beginning of the year 2000, Harland & Wolff and the St-Nazaire yard owned by Alstom were still in the running. The signs were difficult to interpret. The French yard had made its name over the years in the construction of large and luxurious cruise ships and even now it had in progress several units in various stages of building. Harland & Wolff had built no large passenger ship since *Canberra* in 1961, and in recent years had concentrated on oil rigs. Its order books were empty and the survival of the Belfast yard – and with it 2,000 jobs – depended on the Cunard contract.

Micky Arison visited both yards personally on several occasions for negotiations and to receive the suggestions of the would-be builders of the new Cunarder. That he favoured Harland & Wolff may have had little to do with the history of the company or his wish for a British yard to build a British ocean giant. It is also questionable to what extent social considerations played a role. Probably Harland & Wolff gave Cunard/Carnival more room to negotiate because the contract was more important to the Ulster yard. Ultimately finance was decisive. Apart from the deposit, it is the custom for the shipyard to foot the bill until the ship is finally accepted. In the case of 'Project Queen Mary' the cost was estimated at $700 million. This was more than Harland & Wolff could manage. A government credit was necessary but the assurance was too long in coming. Since the Ulster bid exceeded the French one by $118 million, on 9 March 2000 Cunard signed a Letter of Intent with Chantiers de l'Atlantique at St-Nazaire.

Larry Pimentel, Micky Arison and Patrick Boissiers, Chairman of the French yard, now revealed further details of the project and the ship's name: *Queen Mary 2*. 'QM2 will measure over 1,130 feet in length,' Pimentel said. 'That's just 117 feet shorter than the Empire State Building is tall. She'll tower nearly 21 stories in height from keel to masthead, with a gross registered tonnage of nearly 150,000 tons.' Boissier, who had succeeded in bringing Chantiers from the edge of bankruptcy to its status as a major world shipyard within a few

short years, said, 'We want to build this magnificent ship because of our history and because of our future. We understand the character of the ship they want to build, and we know how to build that kind of ship.'

Until the final signing of contracts there remained still a few months during which Stephen Payne and his team worked to perfect their design. Its details were available to shipyard staff while the Carnival management worked on peripheral data. The agreed sum was eventually $780 million, and the commissioning date was set for the end of 2003. With a passenger capacity of 'only' 2,620, the guests would have a new sensation of roominess, since no other ship anywhere made so much space per passenger available. The basic technical specifications were also set out for the first time. 'From the time we first considered purchasing Cunard,' Micky Arison explained, 'our plans always included building a new liner. Cunard's tremendous global brand equity was built by many famous

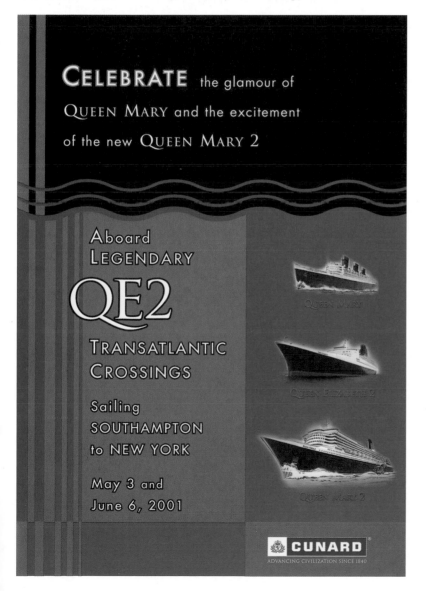

liners and now will be carried on by *Queen Mary 2.*'

'We are extremely pleased to have been selected for one of the most sought-after and highly anticipated shipbuilding contracts in modern-day cruising,' Patrick Boissier added, '*Queen Mary 2* will be a piece of history and a work of art, and perhaps the world's most famous liner even before she sails.' Finally Larry Pimentel announced that at 135 feet in the beam, *QM2* would be too wide to pass through the Panama Canal, but he hoped that in the course of the decade the canal would be widened to accommodate ships of that size. His hopes were met: in a referendum in October 2006 the majority of the Panamanian electorate voted for the locks to be widened to 180 feet. For Larry Pimentel it was by then of no importance – at least not as Chairman of Cunard. In February 2001 he resigned with immediate effect, explaining that his decision had been brought about by the inroads his work was making on his family life. Unofficially, differences between Pimentel and the Carnival Corporation management were hinted at. Pamela Conover, born of British parents in Bangkok, who had been Cunard's Chief Operations Officer since 1998, was nominated as his successor with

immediate effect.

Soon afterwards Stephen Payne's work stood its first real test. Two 'true-to-scale' models of *QM2* with drive had been made for the test tanks. These were important because although the design above the waterline was based on decades of experience with ships in the North Atlantic, below the waterline there were some grey areas. In contrast to the rather box-form underbelly of modern cruise ships, in designing the underwater part of the hull Payne had followed the nautical requirements of a liner. The massive bulge at the forefoot preceded a fine, elongated streamlining providing little resistance and acceptable hydrodynamics despite high speed and deep draught. This provides good sea-keeping qualities in which the ship parts the waves instead of 'surfing' them. In order to protect the liner against following seas, Payne favoured the traditional rounded cruiser stern. Here a compromise had to be found because a broad, flat ship's bottom was necessary for the modern propeller 'pods' mounted below the hull. The solution was a relatively box-shaped after-ship with a cruiser stern 'welded on'. Critics saw this as a deficiency because the seam at the hull side is not flowing but has a 'kink'. Nevertheless the cruiser stern, though interpreted as an experiment with classic style elements, was chosen for its function.

The choice for the model tests was the maritime research institute MARIN at Wageningen in the Netherlands. Its test basin is forty-one feet long, 130 feet wide and sixteen feet deep. The institute is equipped to simulate almost any kind of sea conditions true to scale so that potential weaknesses in ship design can be recognised and corrected before construction begins. In the long and expensive tests the two *QM2* models exhibited excellent sea-keeping qualities. Roll movements were effectively eliminated by the four stabilisers (two on each side of the ship). The slender hull parted the waves outstandingly and even storm-whipped

Pamela C Conover, Cunard President, 2001–4

CUNARD

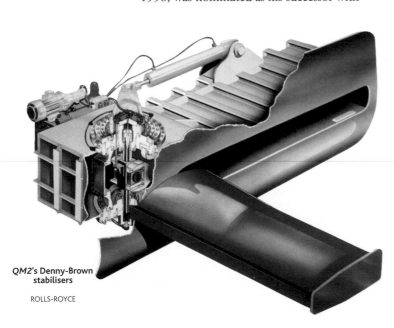

QM2's Denny-Brown stabilisers

ROLLS-ROYCE

seas seemed to cause *QM2* no difficulties. The tests also brought important confirmation that the constellation of propeller pods was viable. Stephen Payne had chosen pod drive, which had been tested in the past but had not undergone long-term trials.

A 'pod' consists of an electric motor housed in a streamlined gondola outside the ship's hull. The propeller is connected directly to the motor by a short shaft. The gondolas are usually so fitted that they can turn through 360 degrees around their vertical axis. This renders the traditional ship's rudders superfluous because the direction of travel is controlled by the set of the pods. In order to drive the enormous mass of the world's greatest liner with its almost thirty-three-foot draught at thirty knots, Payne had calculated that two propellers would be inadequate. *QM2* required four propellers (or four pods). The two sternmost inner pods revolve and also function as rudders while the outermost pods located a few yards forward of them are fixed and used only for propulsion. Here the model tests revealed one of the few

weaknesses in Payne's design. In a following sea the stern of the *QM2* models began to pitch uncontrollably, showing that in rough seas the propellers were likely to leave the water. This phenomenon was cured by placing a fin between the two forward pods, and after this *QM2* completed all her tests successfully.

Four sixteen-cylinder diesels (Type 16V46C-CR EnviroEngine) supplied by the Finnish manufacturer Wärtsilä generate the electrical power driving the pod motors. Originating from collaborations between Wärtsilä and the Carnival Corporation, the EnviroEngine in its variants is today one of the most successful ship engines and is fully proven in other fields ashore, such as energy production. Each of the *QM2* diesels is about forty-one feet long and eighteen feet high, weighs 214 tons and has an output of 16.8 Megawatts (about 22,800hp). The EnviroEngine is especially environmentally friendly, and is almost smoke-free, so the manufacturer states. This is achieved by electronically regulated 'Common-Rail-Injection'. In a common supply system for all cylinders, fuel is maintained at a constant high temperature before injection into the cylinder and then injected electronically into the combustion chamber as required. To reduce dangerous exhaust gases (mainly carbon dioxide and nitrogen oxide) between the working strokes, water injected into the cylinder is vaporised by the high temperatures before entry into the combustion chamber, so reducing the production of nitrogen oxide by up to 60 per cent. A further advantage of this kind of engine is the wide selection of fuel, from cheap bunker oil C to biodiesel. Generators coupled to the EnviroEngines convert the output into electrical energy, which is then led off to the drive pods under the broad upsweep of the ship's bottom astern.

For the new Cunarder the Rolls-Royce Mermaid type was decided upon, probably because its DC motors were built by Alstom,

The diesel engines of *QM2* consume 72 tons of ship's diesel oil daily. If the turbines are coupled in for high speed, these consume an additional 144 tons of expensive gas oil daily. Even that is economical compared with the 600 tons of ship's oil which the engines of the first *Queen Mary* consumed daily on the North Atlantic run

Four Wärtsilä-EnviroEngines are the heart of the *QM2*'s engine-room

WÄRTSILÄ FINLAND OY

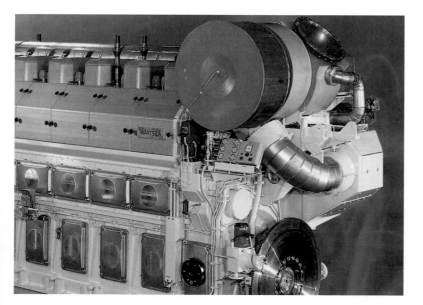

which controls Chantiers de l'Atlantique. Each of the four units weighs 250 tons and has a fixed-blade propeller facing forward. The ship is therefore drawn forward by its propellers and not pushed as with traditional screws. Unusually the *QM2* propellers are made of stainless steel. The angle of each blade is fixed, and in the event of damage only individual blades have to be changed and not the whole propeller. Several of these blades are displayed like a piece of artwork on the foredeck between the wave-deflector and the bridge facing, in an area accessible to passengers.

The four 21.5MW (about 29,200hp) Mermaid pods are among the most powerful units of this kind anywhere on a passenger ship. This kind of power plant dispenses with the long propeller shafts of conventional drive and minimises energy loss caused by friction. The main engines which produce the current for the pod motors can be placed wherever convenient in the ship's hull to enable the most favourable centre of gravity to be chosen. Having the propulsion units out of the hull reduces noise and vibration in the ship. Finally, the need for

special plating around the shaft housing from where the shafts emerge in traditional ships is also dispensed with, and the underwater hull astern can be shaped flat.

A traditional rudder is only effective with a certain forward motion of the ship, and even then a large part of the stream does not flow in the required direction. Since the pods (in the case of *QM2* two of them) can be made to revolve freely about the vertical axis, the water stream can be diverted in any desired direction. This results in better course stability and – in combination with the bow-thrusters – greatly improved manoeuvrability. Thus despite her enormous bulk *QM2* is much less dependent on tug assistance than *QE2* with her traditional propulsion.

The combination of the EnviroEngines with the Mermaid pods gives the *QM2* enough power to provide the required twenty-four to twenty-five knots for the North Atlantic line service. Higher speeds – up to a maximum of thirty knots – call for more power, which aboard *QM2* is generated by two General Electric Type LM 2500+ gas turbines. These are similar to aircraft

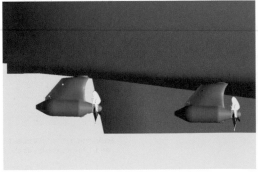

Each Mermaid pod of the QM2 weighs 250 tons – about the same as an Airbus A340

AIRBUS SAS, ROLLS-ROYCE

Schematic representation of the pods fitted to the underwater section of QM2's hull. Note the central fin to improve sea-keeping quality

ROLLS-ROYCE

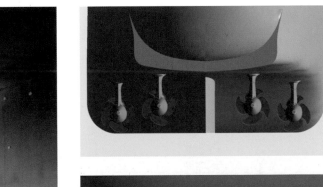

Evolution of the restaurant on the *QE2*'s quarter-deck: as the Columbia Restaurant in 1990 top left
and 1986 top right, as the Mauretania Restaurant in 1995 and as the Caronia Restaurant in 2002

PHOTOS TOP AND CENTRE: ANDREW KILK. PHOTOS BELOW: AUTHOR

turbines. Their great demand for air would require an expensive system of feed piping were they to be installed in the hull, so the turbines are located in a sound-proofed room at the rear of the funnel.

The turbines are coupled to the generators through a reduction gearing. At 3,600 revolutions per minute a further 50MW (about 68,000hp) can be generated, but in regular operations of *QM2* the use of gas turbines is the exception rather than the rule. The power output of the machinery is such that if the *QM2* were used as a power station she would generate enough electrical power to fulfil the needs of a city the size of Southampton.

After the successful test-tank trials with the *QM2* models, the next twelve months were taken up with improving the blueprints, ordering materials and preparing designs for the interior fittings – mostly behind closed doors. Mention of the *QM2* now appeared regularly in prospectuses and on the official Cunard Line Internet site. Establishment of the new Cunard image – the corporate identity – had gone ahead smoothly after the takeover by Carnival. As previously mentioned, *Vistafjord* had been renamed *Caronia* in 1999 after renovation and had reappeared in December that year in the new livery and with her saloons restructured, so abolishing her Norwegian character in favour of a modern interpretation of the British look. During the renovation numerous public rooms (eg the Franconia Restaurant, the White Star Bar and the Piccadilly Club) had received new names recalling the history of Cunard. More investment had also gone into *QE2* to modernise areas untouched during the previous overhaul. A few years previously the Mauretania and Caronia Restaurants had changed names. The Caronia Restaurant described in Chapter 2 had not proved successful as the dining hall for the expensive categories of cabin. Its design was too large, too complex and too cold in its conception, and it was thus renamed Mauretania

Restaurant, while the 'new' Caronia Restaurant was to be given a first-class interior. Cunard contracted the Swedish firm Tillberg Design to recreate the inner saloons on both *QE2* and *Caronia*. There was a publicity angle behind the choice, for Tillberg was one of two firms awarded a contract to furnish the *QM2*; passengers on the two remaining Cunard ships would therefore have a foretaste of the opulence to be expected of *QM2*.

In 1999 *QE2* celebrated her thirtieth year in service. When about to enter Lloyd Werft at Bremerhaven for overhaul, she became the target of the environmental protection group Greenpeace. Off Bremerhaven, thirty activists in seven inflatable dinghies intercepted the liner in the Weser estuary in order to draw attention to the environmental threat caused by ships' anti-fouling paints containing the ingredient TBT (Tributylzinn). According to Greenpeace this chemical is one of the most lethal long-term poisons identified in all the worlds' oceans. The harbour mud at Lloyd Werft was particularly highly impregnated with TBT. Greenpeace succeeded in spraying the words 'God Save the Queen from TBT' along the side of the moving ship while other activists using floats, canoes and swimmers prevented *QE2* from entering the shipyard. Others protested with flags and banners. The situation was tense, for not only was the demonstration bad publicity for the ship, but every minute's delay was financially costly for Lloyd Werft, whose timetable for the renovation work was extremely tight. Upon receipt of Cunard's promise to use TBT-free anti-fouling in future the tension deflated and *QE2* entered the yard the same day. Besides the usual repair work, the Tillberg design was realised aboard during the three-week stay. The most important change was the redesigned Caronia Restaurant. The 554-guest saloon received a half-rounded, slightly raised entry podium by which diners descended two steps into the full-size gourmet restaurant. The

CLOCKWISE
Of all the areas aboard *QE2*, the Queens Room has changed least

ANDREW KILK 1986, 1992, 1995, AUTHOR'S COLLECTION 2002

furniture and wood panelling were of mahogany; large crown-lights in the white ceiling, indirect lighting and dark red carpeting provided the noble atmosphere of a British ancestral hall. Later, passengers acclaimed the new decor of the restaurant, which now truly merited the title 'dining hall'. The renovated Queens Room was similarly admired. The basic scheme of the saloon with its Formica columns and mahogany panelling was retained for the formal atmosphere. The cube-shaped leather armchairs – a relic of the 1980s – were replaced by comfortable blue and gold cushioned chairs, and the floor given a soft blue carpet patterned with gold Tudor roses. Numerous other rooms were recarpeted, and the bathrooms, which had escaped the 1994 overhaul, renovated. When *QE2* sailed on her last transatlantic passage of

1999 her adoring public were unanimous that 'their ship' had never looked so good.

Not quite two years later, on 11 September 2001, terrorists hijacked four US passenger aircraft and created an inferno which will remain for ever in the memories of those who witnessed it. One of the machines was intended to crash dive into the Pentagon. A second crashed into a field in Pennsylvania after passengers overcame the hijackers. The other two aircraft hit the twin towers of the World Trade Center office block in New York. Millions worldwide watched in horror as one of the symbols of New York City collapsed like a pack of cards, covering south Manhattan in a cloud of dust, smoke and fear. Over the next few days the world waited anxiously for what might follow.

Cunard was now confronted by a problem

requiring an urgent solution: both *QE2* and *Caronia* were due in New York on 16 September, the former at the end of an Atlantic crossing, *Caronia* from a cruise to Bermuda. Arriving in New York was out of the question: the city was in a state of emergency and hotel beds were in very short supply, being needed for the rescue and salvage services. Telephones at Cunard were never silent, arranging the diversions to Boston, booking hotel accommodation in the city and organising transport from New York to Boston for the next batch of passengers. Finally, forward passengers had to be advised that for the next five weeks Boston and not New York would act as the American host to the Cunard Line. The next three voyages of *QE2* to the USA ended at the Black Falcon Cruise Terminal in Boston.

On 7 January 2002 *QE2* made her first call to New York after the terrorist attacks, being the first large passenger ship to return to the Hudson. Off Ground Zero the ship stopped to pay respects to the dead and a wreath was cast into the waters. The events of 11 September had not only logistical but also financial repercussions, for here was proof how easy it was to hijack an aircraft even in the era of modern control methods. The fear of flying which resulted led above all in the United States to a wave of cancellations of holiday bookings, which ultimately affected all cruise-ship companies, for especially Americans living inland far from the sea used internal flights to reach departure ports, while cruise ships were now also recognised as potential targets for terrorist attack. For a short while the whole tourist industry suffered under this phenomenon, and for some it was a death sentence. Renaissance Cruises, for example, founded in 1989, had borrowed heavily to expand its fleet. The financial structure of the organisation held for as long as passengers paid for their booked voyages. Cancellations and reluctance to book ahead forced the company into liquidation only a fortnight after 9-11.

While the image of the burning twin towers was not easily erased, its effect on tourism was not enduring. Even immediately after the event, Carnival Corporation's receipts were up to the extent that at the beginning of 2002 new bookings reached a record level. Because of its strong financial position, the financial market did not consider Carnival endangered although there was speculation to that effect when building work began on *QM2*. Just as the short-lived crisis in aviation had consequences for shipping companies, this had a knock-on effect for the shipbuilding industry. In view of the possible collapse of the tourist industry, shipbuilding orders were held back, options extended and acceptance dates postponed. Chantiers de l'Atlantique had no direct link to Renaissance Cruises, but the mother company Alstom had given Renaissance a $1.4 billion credit to build eight medium-large R-Class ships. Despite the Alstom board's assurance that it had insurance cover for the eventuality, this kind of difficulty often tended to persist, the financial world was not happy with the assurance, and Alstom shares fell to their lowest-ever level on the Paris Stock Exchange.

If its industrial concerns including Chantiers de l'Atlantique had gone under, that would have meant the end of the *QM2* project. Micky Arison, who was not interested in shipbuilding but only in having his luxury liner built, stated that the Carnival Corporation and its subsidiaries had $1.2 billion available for investment plus $1.6 billion in credits should the need arise. By this he meant that Carnival had the means to support the shipyard until it sorted out its finances or finished building the *QM2*, and to emphasise his strengths he brought forward the starting date by six weeks. In a small ceremony on 16 January 2002 the Cunard President and Managing Director, Pamela Conover, set in motion the machine with which the first piece of steel for the new ocean leviathan was cut. 'It has been pointed out to me', Miss Conover said, 'that the one surefire way to guarantee that a ship is completed on time is to make sure that the chairman of the shipyard is booked together *with his wife* on the maiden voyage,' at which she handed Patrick Boissier two tickets for the first voyage of *QM2*.

Nowadays a ship is assembled in dock from prefabricated elements rather as if she were just an oversize model. The time when the keel was laid on a slipway, and frames, plating and gradually all parts and the hull were bolted or welded together, is long past. The ship grew in

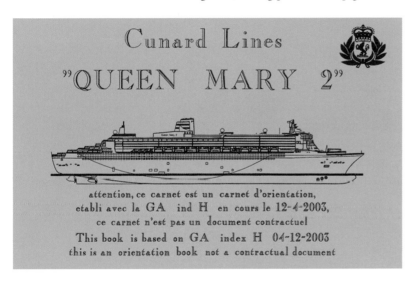

Extract from the General Plan for G32 which served as a workers' guide

ALSTOM – CHANTIERS DE L'ATLANTIQUE, STEFAN BEHN COLLECTION

painstakingly small stages, mounted piece by piece from below to above. The modern ship grows from midships to astern, forwards and upwards at the same time, and on completion the dock is flooded and the ship floats. A traditional launch, in which the heavy steel hull trundles down the slip into the water, now occurs seldom.

The Chantiers de l'Atlantique shipyard consists of several assembly halls in which parts of the ship are fabricated. The *QM2* construction plan laid down precisely the size, hardness and shape of the steel needed for individual areas of the ship. Especially in the hull of a transatlantic liner, few plates are perfectly flat. For the bow and stern special machines are required which use pressure and

heat to press and roll to the final form. With the symbolic first step Miss Conover set off a process in which cutting and working the steel would be the daily task for the next eighteen months. Cranes using electro magnets transported the prefabricated steel from dockyard warehouses to yard workshops to be made into 'panels' containing cable and air-shafts, water piping and so forth. In the next, pre-production stage, panels are assembled into larger units or 'blocks'. These are fitted with auxiliary machinery, bathrooms, etc and, depending on the intended place of installation and weight limitations, are lifted by crane aboard many-wheeled shipyard transporters of remarkable manoeuvrability and taken from the Pre-Production Hall to the edge of the building dock for warehousing.

Dry Dock B at the yard is 3,000 feet long and 200 feet wide. It has been the cradle for many cruise ships, gas tankers and warships of our time besides the *QM2*. The warehousing for the prefabricated blocks is nearby. The location is straddled by two gigantic cranes 200 feet tall with a lifting capacity of 800 tons. The dock itself is on two levels: the deeper part is at the river end, separated from the waters of the Loire by a sluice gate. About half-way inland is a 'step' several yards high.

A new construction always begins in Dock B on the upper level. The great cranes lift the blocks from the warehouse to the dock and deposit them on the wooden support beams which bear the weight of the developing hull.

In modern shibuilding procedure this corresponds to the traditional 'keel-laying', and so on 4 July 2002, six months after work began, the leading personalities of the undertakings involved celebrated this important occasion in the building of the ocean giant known to the yard as 'G32'. With Patrick Boissier, Pamela Conover and Micky Arison were Captain Ronald W Warwick, who would become a living legend among Cunard captains. The date was chosen especially to recall the opening of the

North Atlantic liner service 162 years before by Sir Samuel Cunard aboard RMS *Britannia*. On this day another milestone would be passed in the history of the organisation. Captain Warwick was present for publicity purposes. As the designated Master of *QE2*, his late father Commodore William E Warwick had once watched over the construction of the new liner at the John Brown & Co yard. In 1990 Warwick Jr had taken over the bridge of the Cunard flagship. Of imposing stature, with white beard and blue eyes, he was the picture-book image of a ship's captain, and just as many passengers thought the Master of a great ocean liner should look. As Cunard's longest-serving captain, and on account of the good reputation he enjoyed with passengers and colleagues, he was the Line's first choice to occupy the post of Master of the *QM2*. Like his father before him he spent the last months before the commissioning of his new ship at the dockyard in order to familiarise himself with his new command.

After the usual fine words and publicity

This image of *QM2* under construction illustrates well the modular method of construction in modern shipbuilding

TILLBERG DESIGN AB

The bridge section being lowered aboard

TILLBERG DESIGN AB

Towards the end of 2000 Cunard published this artist's impression of its new flagship, with *QE2* in the background. The detail is remarkable bearing in mind the early date. The artist allowed himself to borrow some details from *QE2*, however, such as the high funnel and rounded stern

CUNARD

material which always accompany such events came the coin-laying ceremony. In the days of sail it was customary to place a coin under each of the masts for good luck. The tradition persists to this day and was continued by Pamela Conover and Patrick Boissier with the new Cunarder. As a symbol of Cunard's nation, Great Britain, Miss Conover placed a commemorative £5 coin marking the Jubilee of Queen Elizabeth II in the section of double-bottom where the assembly of G32 would begin. Patrick Boissier added an old silver 100 franc coin as a symbol of the country of construction, France. Pamela Conover concluded: 'I think it appropriate that the first Master of *QM2* should today issue his first order: the order to lay the section of the keel.' She handed Captain Warwick a radio telephone. He thanked her and said, 'Crane driver, this is Captain Warwick speaking. Please commence the building of my ship.' Seconds later the 650-ton sections of blocks 502 and 503 were lifted into the air and, suspended from strong steel cables, glided to Dock B to be lowered slowly and precisely upon the support beams. A further ninety-six blocks would follow these first two before the ship was complete.

The construction of *QM2* began on the upper level of Dock B. Building dry docks on two levels allows prefabrication and work to proceed on several new ships at the same time. Prefabrication has the additional advantage that the blocks can be assembled in protected areas regardless of the weather. Once the new construction in Dock B reaches the height at which it is difficult for the 200-foot-tall cranes to operate, the incomplete midships section is sealed off fore and aft with steel plating and the dock flooded. The section floats and is towed to the deeper part of the dock to obtain sufficient clearance overhead for the crane gantries to continue. A second new ship can now be started in the vacated upper level.

The incomplete *QM2* hull first floated on 1

December 2002, after which the landward end of the dry dock was free to accommodate construction work on the Mediterranean Shipping Company's new cruise ship *MSC Opera*. The initial phase of work is characterised by high precision and extremely heavy materials. Among the first components to be installed in the hull of G32 were the four Wärtsilä diesels. Because of their size these were best installed early, before many decks towered over the engine-room deep in the ship's interior. Wrapped in blue plastic sheets for protection, the valuable main engines were installed soon after the keel was laid (although technically not correct, this term remains in use for convenience).

The steel giant now began to grow in height and length. Up to 1,500 male and 100 female temporary dockworkers were employed on building the *QM2*. On the bare incomplete decks one saw figures crouched over the sparking of welding tools, and more blocks from the pre-production halls arriving and being lifted over the dock walls. Men with hand radios passed precise instructions to the crane drivers gliding the heavy steel sections to guide rails on the hull for welding in place on the spot.

Meanwhile Cunard was making its commercial preparations for the new flagship. In June 2002 the first voyage destinations of the *QM2* were made known. Cunard also made public the fact that the liner would sail from Southampton on her maiden voyage on 12 January 2004 and – to the disapproval of the traditionalists – this would not be a classic North Atlantic passage but would follow a more southerly route via the Canaries to Fort Lauderdale, Florida.

G32 leaving dock at St-Nazaire on 20 March 2003

CUNARD

At last the construction was sufficiently far advanced for the launching, or at least what passes for it today. 'To launch a ship' has always been understood to mean the act of releasing the readied hull down the inclined stocks into the water – 'to marry the sea' as the former French President Charles de Gaulle expressed it at the launching of the liner *France*. The *QM2* had been built in dry dock without slip or staging. In modern shipbuilding the equivalent of the traditional launching is the technical process of flooding the dock, floating the hull and towing it to the fitting-out quay.

Previously the Loire had been dredged to the appropriate depth and Dry Dock C prepared as the cradle of the new Cunarder. Floating the hull simply to transfer it to another dry dock may seem odd at first glance but has a technical reason. Traditionally the launched hull is taken to the fitting-out quay, where the empty shell will be filled with engines and machinery and the superstructure put on, after which the interior will be fitted out. At her 'launching', *QM2* already had a large proportion of necessities in place in her steel hull, for whereas in the classic launching the hull must be light enough to trundle down the slipway into the water, where 'launching' means floating the hull instead, the weight is irrelevant. The ship can then be fitted out in the preferred technical and logistical sequence.

QM2 had to vacate Dock B to create space to build *MSC Opera* and a liquid-gas tanker, and also because the gantries of the two bridge-cranes did not have the clearance to install the funnel section 236 feet above the keel. The shipyard did not consider *QM2* to be a normal cruise ship but rather treated it as 1.6 ships, and 1.6 ships could not pass through the narrow channel into the Forme Joubert, the shipyard's fitting-out basin. Consequently, for the first time in over twenty years, Dock C had been recommissioned. Built originally as a precaution for the closing of the Suez Canal and the oil

crisis in the early 1970s, between 1976 and 1979 it had seen the construction of four *Batillus*-Class tankers of 555,000 tons deadweight and 1,358 feet long, but since then the giant dock had languished. Strictly speaking the Forme Joubert is not a true dock, for although it has walls, a sluice gate and a bottom of reinforced-steel concrete, it is actually a giant pool in the ground. After two decades of inactivity it had to be emptied and cleared of many years' accumulated fouling. The concrete floor was damaged and required replacement. With new support beams tailor-made for the *QM2* it was soon ready to receive the luxury liner.

To continue fitting out *QM2* in dry dock proved fortunate, for during the planning period of the new Cunarder, cruise ships fitted with pod-drive were still in their infancy. Long-term trials were still in hand and had shown that the innovation was not without its problems. The system was excellent for cargo vessels, which spend much longer periods at sea and less time in port, but when it was fitted to cruise ships with almost daily tight manoeuvring, metal fatigue had been detected. The four sister ships of the Millennium Class built at Chantiers had had endless difficulties with them. The four Mermaid pods of G32 were inspected and weaknesses found. Two pods were shipped back to Rolls-Royce in Norway while the others were modified at Nancy, France. Thus *QM2* left dry dock without her pods, which were later fitted in Dock C.

While the successive milestones in the construction of G32 were marked by celebrations, the 'launching' (in earlier times a high spot in the building stage of a ship) had the character of a purely technical procedure. On the night of 20 March 2003 Dock B was flooded and *QM2* rose from the support beams. At 0543 she was towed out of the dock by four tugs, a spectacular sight. The underwater hull had been given two coats of anti-fouling paint, which was visible only by a narrow red stripe at the

One of the numerous pieces of art supplied by Onderneming & Konst

AUTHOR

Frank Symeou and Mark Lightowler of the London firm 'designteam' designed many of the ship's interior rooms

DESIGNTEAM

waterline. Above it the gigantic body of the ship towered steely-grey towards the heavens. Emergency generators aboard provided lighting, and the windows of the colossus glowed eerily in the early morning mist. At 0720 *QM2* made fast in Dock C, where she would remain for the next six months until her sea trials.

While the outer structure up to funnel level was virtually complete, work continued on the technical fittings and internal construction. Three firms were given charge of the saloon furbishings. Tillberg Design AB of Helsingborg, Sweden, devoted its creative energies to 80 per cent of these areas. The company, founded in 1960 by its proprietor Robert Tillberg, had developed from modest beginnings, working on the internal decor of freighters and Baltic ferries, and had an impressive portfolio of shore work, graphic designs and especially decor work on cruise ships. The first was *Kungsholm*, built at John Brown & Co immediately before *QE2*; then came the 'Love Boat' *Sea Venture*, the renovation of *Vistafjord* and *Sagafjord* in the early 1990s, *Oriana*, built for P&O in Germany, and the renovation of the *QE2* with her impressive Caronia Restaurant, already described, other recent large cruise ships, and the pretentious Baltic ferry *Color Fantasy*. Tillberg Design also has offices in London and at the cruise-ship centre in Miami, where the proximity to Cunard and Carnival must be an advantage.

In January 1998, just a few months before 'Project Queen Mary' was announced, the London firm 'designteam' was founded. It received the remaining 20 per cent of the orders for the *QM2*'s decor. The founders of this young firm, Frank Symeou and Eric Mouzourides, already had ten years' experience in the decor of large cruise ships, and within a short time of founding 'designteam' they won contracts to fit out several public rooms on Voyager and Radiance Class ships for Royal Caribbean International and Celebrity Cruise's Millennium

Development of the Grand Lobby created by Tillberg, from its earliest design (right, February 2002) to a computer graphic used by Cunard for publicity purposes (below), and the finished product (opposite)

RIGHT: TILLBERG DESIGN AB, BELOW AND OPPOSITE, CUNARD

This bronze relief (above) by the Scot John McKenna is an interpretation of a similar design aboard the first *Queen Mary* (left)

CUNARD

Class. The jewel in the crown is now, as then, the *QM2*.

The third company was immediately involved in the furbishing of the *QM2* and the final decoration of the finished public rooms. The Dutch firm Onderneming & Konst was given a budget of $5 million to provide the *QM2* with works of art. Consisting of five art historians, this organisation acted in a specialist advisory capacity, choosing from a range of artists whose style and craft it considered appropriate. Over fifteen years the organisation had selected paintings, sculpture and reliefs for many offices, numerous cruise ships and several ships of Carnival's Holland America Line. A total of 128 artists contributed work to decorate the *QM2*; of particular interest for passengers with a maritime interest are the oil paintings of the British artist Stephen Card, and other pictures of famous Cunard and White Star liners were hung in stairways and lifts. Hundreds of originals are aboard together with many thousands of prints which decorate cabins and less-well-frequented corners of the ship.

Let us now take the opportunity to tour *QM2* for a look at these creations. If one boards the ship at Southampton, this will usually be by the portside amidships. A broad corridor leads into the Grand Lobby, the 'heart' of *QM2*, responsible every year for providing many thousands of passengers with their first impression of the ship. This area was therefore of especial importance for Tillberg Design. Those who know the interior arrangement of American cruise ships can imagine how difficult intermixing might be to satisfy the tastes of those from both sides of the Atlantic. Cunard and the *QM2* are usually associated with tradition, luxury, breathtaking size, international flair and art deco but also the latest technology. The Grand Lobby is the perfect synthesis, and the impressive atrium is synonymous with a great passenger liner.

This reception area impresses by its spaciousness, a promise that the interior architecture of the ship will have been lavish with space. It extends over two tiers, the passenger entering from ashore by the lower one. The atrium rises through three further decks altogether. This Grand Lobby awakens memories of the great luxury liners of the 1930s while remaining modern. Elegant décor, with tall pseudo-marble columns, provides a tremendous impression, and glass balustrades and mahogany handrails contrast perfectly with the patterned red carpet. The lighting effect seems to lend the hall grandure and sets a glittering background for the great occasion of an Atlantic crossing. Sofas and armchairs are set out on the lower level. Guests requiring assistance seek help at the service counter of the Purser's Office. The great centrepiece of the Grand Lobby is a double stairway leading from the upper level to Deck 2. This satisfies the need to 'see and be seen' every evening when ladies in cocktail dresses and gentlemen in tuxedos descend here like opera stars. The cars of two panoramic glass lifts rise from Deck 2 upwards through the entire Atrium to even higher levels. The space of the Atrium itself is cleverly used, for the windows of many interior cabins look down on the Grand Lobby. On the forward wall of this area is John McKenna's impressive bronze relief, which sets the *QM2* on a compass-rose against a backdrop of an Atlantic chart. The impressive and very wide corridor that leads sternwards from the Grand Lobby is the central passage to the Britannia Restaurant. Red carpeted and wood panelled, it seems to shine in the spotlights.

Our tour from the Grand Lobby takes us forward through a narrower version of the corridor described above, which leads directly to an oversize portrait of Samuel Cunard. It is actually made as a mosaic of Cunard steamships of the last 160 years. On either side of the portrait are the entrances to the Royal Court Theater,* which like the Atrium is on two levels.

*On board a British ship, of course, one would expect the British spelling 'theatre', not the American 'theater'. However, with the exception of 'The Daily Programme', Americanised spelling of English is adopted aboard ship. On board the less cosmopolitan but very British *Queen Victoria*, however, a 'Theatre' is to be found.

The Royal Court Theater under construction and after completion

TILLBERG DESIGN AB, CUNARD

On Deck 2 is the great auditorium, with a balcony on the deck above. The Royal Court Theater can accommodate up to 1,100 guests seated on long red velvet sofas or in revolving chairs with small drinks tables. The Showlounge is a bag of tricks. The revolving stage can be divided into segments of varying height and the orchestra pit raised to the level of the auditorium. Most shows and theatrical plays are performed by members of London's famous and traditional theatrical school, the Royal Academy of Dramatic Art. This arrangement provides the

QM2 with a theatrical troupe at low cost (for the most part it is still in training), and the members of the troupe receive an important reference early in their careers.

The *QM2* has close links with many luxury goods manufacturers, a business strategy which Pamela Conover's 'right hand', the late Deborah Natansohn, introduced to Cunard. Stocking the ship with brand names which clients associate with high-value luxury articles is an additional inducement to book passages, while *QM2* is a powerful piece of advertising for the brand names. Commercial advertising is almost as old as the luxury liner itself. In 1905 the Hamburg-Amerika Line under its then Managing Director Albert Ballin offered its first-class passengers the Ritz-Carlton Restaurant, which was established aboard in the same style as the Paris and London hotels of that name. The Vinolia Otto Toilet Soap Co was proud to announce in 1911 that its produce was distributed in the luxury apartments aboard the White Star liner *Olympic*. In modern business 'networking' the trend is naturally much greater, as we shall observe from

'Illuminations' is the first-ever seaborne planetarium and offers seats for 493 guests. A great dome in the ceiling can be lowered as a screen for six projectors located under Plexiglas cupolas in the viewing room. The room is also available for use as an additional cinema or stage. Its tulip-shaped lamps, pilasters on the walls and red-honey-coloured seating are a modern interpretation of art deco and might have been inspired by decor aboard the French super-liner *Normandie*.

The way through Deck 3L leads back to the Royal Court Theater foyer, but following the stairs to Deck 3 one proceeds astern into the upper level of the Grand Lounge, surrounded on all four sides by the Mayfair Shops, the *QM2* 'shopping mall'. Jewellers rub shoulders with small, exquisite boutiques and a relatively large souvenir shop, a branch of Harrods. The interior design of the latter's world-famous London shopping temple, by the way, is nowadays a Tillberg creation, whereas the shops aboard *QM2* are by 'designteam'.

The Veuve Cliquot Champagne Bar is on the starboard side and represents another 'co-branding' partnership: the *QM2* was named using a bottle of Veuve Cliquot. A broad, imposing corridor, its walls adorned with yard-long art reliefs, leads astern from the Grand Lobby. At sea this area is frequently used for impromptu sales in which long tables are set up to sell jewellery, souvenirs or perfume at reduced prices. Although this 'flea market' is always well attended, it seems odd in a luxury liner. There is a bar on each side of this corridor. Portside is Sir Samuel's Wine Bar, one of the quieter locations among the public rooms. Parquet flooring, a wall painting, furniture in pastel shades and the countenance of the founder of the Line in black on silver bestow a rather reserved elegance. This is a good place for a small group to enjoy quiet, refined conversation over a glass of wine and end the day with a 'chaser'. Starboard side is the Chart Room, one of various rooms named for its

One of the Mayfair Shops

CUNARD

Sir Samuel's Wine Bar

CUNARD

other examples during our tour of *QM2*.

Leaving the Royal Court Theater, short staircases lead to Deck 3L, a 'tween deck between Decks 2 and 3. Since the theatre extends on two levels from port to starboard, Stephen Payne installed a corridor below the seating of the theatre's upper level, creating a passage at half the height of Deck 2. This was done to avoid compelling passengers to make long detours over stairways. From the red-carpeted Grand Lobby and Royal Court Theater one now passes to the beige and brown tones of the conference rooms and auditorium 'Illuminations', the work of 'designteam'.

The Chart Room

CUNARD

The Queens Room's dance-floor is the largest at sea

CUNARD

more attractive. Astern on this deck is the upper entrance to the Britannia Restaurant, the largest room aboard. Its grandeur and elegance awaken memories of the huge dining halls of the ocean liners of days long gone. A breath of art deco, successfully combined with a fresh, modern arrangement, provides a timeless impression and it is difficult to imagine that in twenty years it could look outmoded.

Passengers dine here on three levels: the lower part of the room, on Deck 2, extends across the full beam of the ship. The upper part on Deck 3 circles the Britannia Restaurant in the form of a gallery, whose outer reaches are situated even higher. While this evokes the impression of

counterpart on the *QE2*. Yet while the original is a calm place which tends to become rather noisy, the *QM2* Chart Room is not really convincing. With its pastel-shade patterned grey carpet and silver-grey easy chairs, by day this long saloon has a slightly dusty-looking atmosphere. Under evening spotlights it does tend to resemble a yacht club, but even so the Chart Room lacks small intimate nooks to make it that little bit

small, private sectors, it uses a technique also seen in the Royal Court Theater, for one can reach the stern through a hidden corridor between Deck 2 and Deck 3 on either side of the ship without having to pass through the restaurant. The high ceiling in the centre of the restaurant is supported by ivory double columns. Rather like a celestial vault, the glass ceiling of light blue tint is a light source by night,

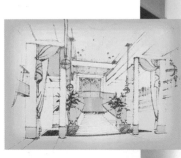

From the study to the 'finalised' computer graphic and the room as it is – the Britannia Restaurant

ABOVE (UPPER)
TILLBERG DESIGN AB,
ABOVE (LOWER) AND RIGHT
CUNARD

This design sketch reveals that the G32 disco was originally conceived as a distinguished yacht club

CUNARD

It is open to discussion whether the Britannia Restaurant aboard *QM2* is so named because it is large enough to house the first Cunard ship RMS *Britannia* completely

spotlights and elegant crown light contributing to the perfect illumination. Various tones of wood trim dominate the walls and furnishings; the upper gallery is surrounded by a balustrade of reinforced glass. A double stairway curves down to the forward end of the dining saloon below so that here one can celebrate the 'grand entrance' in the tradition of past ages – 'see and be seen'.

The dominating focal point is a gigantic tapestry by the Dutch artist Barbara Broekman. The design shows an ocean liner – a synthesis of the first *Queen Mary* and *Queen Mary 2* – before the skyline of Manhattan. Acknowledging the industrial elements in art deco, there is a stylised section of Brooklyn Bridge. Streamers and bright colours give the composition a festive look.

The Britannia Restaurant itself is designed in flowing forms. The blue carpets of the stairways suggest flowing water, on which one 'flows' into the lower saloon. A blue carpet with striking, bright mussel decor recalls a water surface in

motion. Those guests shown to the favoured tables at the sides of the restaurant can actually see water – through great panoramic windows. The Britannia Restaurant can accommodate 1,347 guests, about half the passenger capacity of the ship, so that there have to be two sittings for dinner.

Leaving the upper area of the restaurant for the stern, one finds the night life through a vestibule into the Queens Room, a ballroom which too is named after the example in the *QE2*. Although the Queens Room occupies only one deck, the raised ceiling in the centre enlarges the room to give the impression of a pompous ballroom. Two crown lights are set into the high ceiling, below which is a large wooden dance-floor patterned with a compass rose. At the back is an orchestra stage which can be concealed by a heavy royal blue curtain bearing in gold the letter 'Q'. The ceiling is supported by columns, the dance-floor bordered by yellow-gold and carmine-red easy chairs with small cocktail tables on a slightly raised level to give an unobstructed view of the floor. This room is used during the day for dancing lessons, traditional afternoon tea and musical presentations. Because of its size, the Queens Room is suitable for receptions with large numbers of people and much activity – for example the Captain's reception.

Sternwards beyond the Queens Room is the last room on the deck, simply named 'G32' after the ship's yard number. In 1969 *QE2* had two night-clubs, named the 736 Club and the Q4 Room after her yard number and the popular designation for the *QE2* respectively. Thus G32 aboard *QM2* serves the same purpose, as a night-club and disco in which night owls can dance and party to disco classics into the early hours or chat at the bar or mezzanine. The stylised compass rose laid into the dance floor may remind guests that they are aboard a great luxury liner of the twenty-first century, an impression reinforced by the display of prints around the room. With its metallic structure and gaudy colours, G32 looks like a cross between a 1980s discothèque and a factory hall. In the gloom of evening when the dance-floor is swept by strobe lighting this combination is not so noticeable since people will be looking elsewhere.

From G32 one returns via the Queens Room to other regions of the ship, but so as to avoid passing through the Britannia Restaurant, where the second sitting is at dinner, we use Deck 3L to reach the lower level entrance to the restaurant on Deck 2 and the broad red corridor leading into the Grand Lobby.

There are two other small social areas here. Portside as far as the Grand Lobby is the mainly American domain of the Empire Casino with its roulette and blackjack tables and long rows of gambling machines, silent only once port is reached. To starboard is the Golden Lion Pub, which is so called for the same institution aboard *QE2* and which owes its name to the crowned lion in the Cunard crest, holding the world globe in its claws. The pub is a luxurious interpretation of a traditional English pub for British aristocratic voyagers and the American

The Golden Lion Pub is a luxurious interpretation of the typical British street-corner tavern

CUNARD

idea of the Old World: dark wood, a long bar with porcelain pulling handles, heavy leather settees, iron-based tables, old English decor and pints of ale and lager. Pub food is served all day, from burgers to fish and chips. Even a dartboard

is available. Every evening the Golden Lion Pub is a noisy rendezvous to enjoy beer and other drinks and to enjoy regular outbursts of laughter and applause for the karaoke. The only criticism of this room, as with the Chart Room a deck above, is its lack of a snug.

The *QM2* passenger areas are very successful in two respects. They combine opulent grandeur with an atmosphere of well-being. Nowhere did Stephen Payne attempt to minimise the size of the ship, yet the architecture of the inner rooms avoids giving passengers the feeling of overwhelming size in which one can get lost aboard. Even more important for Payne in his planning was a good passenger flow. This succeeded, for in contrast to *QE2*, whose internal layout was a legacy of the originally planned three-class system, to orient oneself in the *QM2* is not difficult, especially with deck plans located at all central points.

From the Golden Lion Pub one returns to the Grand Lobby skirting the Britannia Restaurant, having now seen two of the three decks solely fitted with public rooms. By lift we rise to Deck 7, dedicated to passenger enjoyment and catering. The lift door opens to reveal the King's Court restaurant, a concession to the American way. While it is the European custom to be served at table in upper-class restaurants, many Americans used to self-service find fixed mealtimes and menus a nuisance – a reason for shipping companies to lay on US dinner buffets and freestyle dining. Late risers who miss breakfast in the Britannia or one of the other restaurants, or overlook lunch while reading in a deckchair on deck, can eat at any time of day in the King's Court. Plastic trays are used for self-service, all manner of delicacies being available on the numerous buffet islands. The restaurant has bright tile flooring, dark wood-panelled walls and bright wickerwork furniture. In the evening the King's Court restaurant is divided into four theme restaurants by sliding panels. Variable lighting and staff dress serve to emphasise the subtle differences in decoration.

Each division is individually named: in La Piazza fine Italian food is served; the Lotus Bar attracts friends of the Asian menu, while the less adventurous will find local dishes in the British Carvery. The most exquisite section of the King's Court in the evening is the Chef's Galley with places for only thirty-five, who can watch their meals being prepared. The fact that the King's Court restaurant lies on the passenger thoroughfare to rooms fore and aft could be seen as a disadvantage, but since there is customarily a good deal of movement in self-service restaurants and the table areas are shielded from the gaze of passers-by by the sliding panels this is not problematical. There is a view over the Promenade Deck through glassed niches set in the side walls. Abaft the King's Court are the extended restaurants for the higher-priced cabin categories – the Queen's Grill and Princess Grill, both named after their equivalents aboard *QE2* and no less imposing.

If one follows the route through Deck 7 further forward, one reaches the Winter Garden

Designed and built as an airy refuge: the Winter Garden

CUNARD

The Canyon Ranch Spa Club

CUNARD

Café, one of the quieter rooms on board despite its size. It is a survival of the winter gardens in vogue aboard ocean liners a century before. Of airy and floral appearance with light wickerwork chairs, the winter garden was then a pleasant change from the heavy decor of the other social rooms and, in top-heavy ships, gave a chance to lower the centre of gravity. Accordingly the Winter Garden aboard *QM2* has comfortable wickerwork furniture and potted plants. The floor has a green-patterned carpet and the centre of the room has a circular ceramic surface with a white piano. A fresco on a bright blue background set in the ceiling is in retro art nouveau style. A stylised glass light-cupola hides the presence of six more decks above. A painted-glass backdrop has parrots on palm branches against a black background, illuminated from behind so that the birds' colours come alive and give the Winter Garden the look of a giant aviary. Since this room is rather removed from most activities, it is at least a quiet spot for genteel conversation over a soft drink or a cup of tea, or the right place to relax with a book.

Proceeding forwards one encounters a bright foyer in which the air has the distinct tang of chlorine – a sure sign that we are entering the domains of fitness and wellness. It is another example of co-branding, for the body-care temple aboard *QM2* is run by the American beauty farmers of Canyon Ranch. Whether for massage, manicure, pedicure, a relaxing bath, aromatherapy, thalassotherapy, skin care or a visit to the Finnish sauna or the steam room, for payment of a surcharge (charged to the cabin account), fifty-one employees are on hand in twenty-four different rooms to treat tired bodies and minds. There is a rest-room with comfortable wickerwork chairs and a wonderful view of the sea, and also a fitness centre with thirty-eight modern gymnastic appliances. The Canyon Ranch Spa Club occupies over 20,000 square feet over two decks and is one of the few institutions on the ship where one has to pay extra.

Through wooden doors so heavy that even a hurricane would have difficulty in shifting them we reach the open deck. From Deck 7 the yards ahead is the grey steel wall of the wave-deflector on the forecastle. One nevertheless can enjoy a fine prospect, but for safety reasons only in calm conditions. Access is through a door in the area between the bridge front and wave-deflector. Here the spare blades for the *QM2*'s propellers are battened down inside guard rails. Turning to face astern here one has the spectacular sight of the great upper works, with their dramatic lines topped six decks above by the massive bridge.

From the tunnel around the foreship one re-enters the Promenade Deck. It runs astern for almost 1,000 feet and below the ship's lifeboats. These are ready for lowering from the Promenade Deck in an emergency at a height of ninety feet above sea level. This is an exception to the UN SOLAS (Safety of Life at Sea) Convention, which stipulates a maximum height of fifty feet. Proving that wave heights in excess of fifty feet in the Atlantic are not a rarity, Stephen Payne requested and received approval to position the boats much higher on the *QM2* to reduce the risk of loss or wave damage.

The Promenade Deck impresses by its size, not only in length but also in breadth – four can walk its teak planks abreast and still leave room for people to sprawl in the wooden and green canvas deckchairs with their dark green cushions. Walking sternwards along the Promenade Deck one comes to the terrace-like sun decks. Steps lead below to the Minnows' Pool, reserved for children, who can make as much noise as they please far from the everyday life of the ship. In the interior are two rooms for children of different age groups: the Zone and Play Zone. The colourful rooms have many toys. Two female carers are here all day to ensure that even the youngest passengers enjoy the voyage while parents have time to themselves. Two decks above on Deck 8 is the Terrace Pool, which complements the Minnows' Pool and is for adults only. Like any beach, the large area around the pool is well attended in fine weather

The Play Zone keeps the youngest passengers occupied

CUNARD

A small area of the forecastle deck space – sporting spare propeller blades – is accessible to passengers if weather allows

MARTIN GRANT

superstructure is set back, and so it is here that one can walk all the way round the ship in the open air. The way forward passes through a kind of tunnel with enormous panoramic windows. Irrespective of natural air movement or the winds of passage along the Promenade Deck, this forward end of the superstructure is protected against the weather. The panoramic windows do not offer much of a view, for a few by sun-worshippers.

The view aloft reveals rows of great windows decks higher, spread across the entire breadth of the ship. These super-expensive Duplex and Grand Duplex Suites are the largest aboard. They are named after various estates of the British nobility, and equipped accordingly. The outer Grand Duplexes, 'Balmoral' and 'Sandringham', occupy a huge 2,249 square feet of space each. They extend over two levels, served by a stairway or private lift. The suites

The 'Balmoral' suite occupies 2,249 square feet

CUNARD

have butler service, two baths each with whirlpool, guest bathroom with shower, flat-screen TV, training apparatus, dressing room and a dining room for eight people. The three Duplex apartments, 'Buckingham', 'Windsor' and 'Holyrood', are each 'only' 1,471 square feet These five suites share a private sun deck on Deck 9 – naturally with dividing wall – giving an unobstructed view of the sea and the activities on the sun decks below.

A part of the common sun deck with its Terrace Pool is transformed in warmer climate zones every evening into an extension of the Todd English restaurant, another trade mark of world reputation which co-brands with the *QM2*. The restaurant name itself is the trade mark, a reminder that the *QM2* is not a British thoroughbred like her illustrious predecessors but was built with American money. Though not well known in Europe, Todd English is a culinary giant in the United States – not only a

A view from the raw beginnings of the Terrace Pool on Deck 8 towards the aft superstructure. Suites will be installed soon behind the five great dual openings

DESIGNTEAM

Three stages of development of the Todd English restaurant

ABOVE LEFT AND RIGHT, DESIGNTEAM:
BELOW, CUNARD

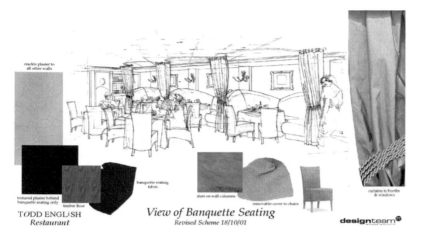

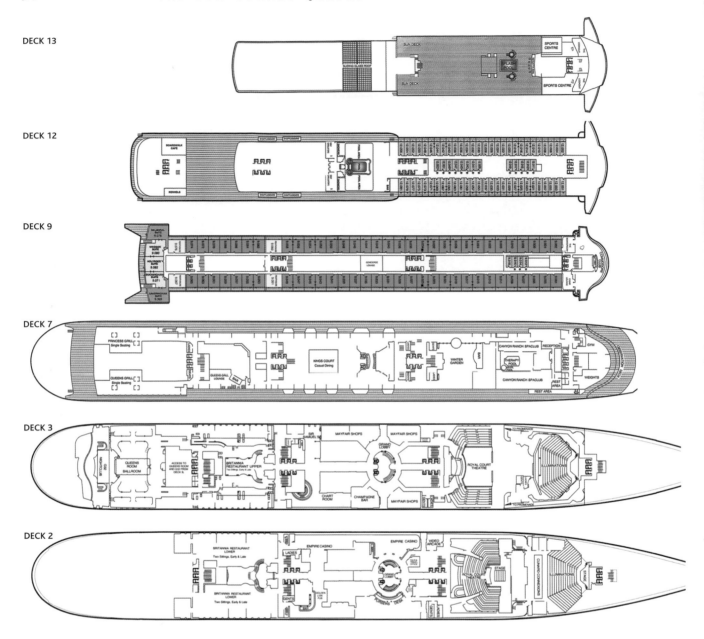

gifted chef who in the fifteen years before the construction of the *QM2* had won a number of prizes for his culinary creations, but also a successful businessman, TV personality and author of three highly praised cookbooks.

English, born in 1960, began his career as a chef at the age of fifteen and in 1982 graduated with an honours degree from the Culinary Institute of America. In 1989 he opened Olives, a gourmet restaurant in Charlestown, Massachusetts, and branches followed all across the United States. Further businesses and TV appearances were followed by the Todd English restaurant aboard *QM2*, whose menus are personally composed by the master. The paying restaurant, a modern copy of the famous Verandah Grills aboard the first two Queens, has space for only 156 guests. Reservations are obligatory and punctuality is advisable. While the *QM2* kitchens are the equal of those of quality restaurants ashore, the Todd English Restaurant is a cut above them.

The correct ambience was created by 'designteam', giving English's Mediterranean-influenced kitchen a Mediterranean-oriental look. In the style of classic dining rooms, the restaurant has a vestibule where guests can gather before dinner. The central element here is the large, red, rounded Ottoman with purple and gold cushions standing on an aubergine-coloured round covering the otherwise grey-patterned carpet. Gold curtains hung from the ceiling and secured in huge gold tassels form a screen to booths and windows in the central banqueting area. Free-floating amphora in picture frames on the wall provide a first idea of the geographic origins of the coming delicacies, bear witness to the avant-garde claim to be a temple of dining, and are slightly ridiculous. The combination of red, aubergine, grey and gold continues into the restaurant, where diners sit at high-backed grey-cushioned chairs or aubergine-coloured long sofas. Between are separating panels in dark grey marbling, while the wall paintings in over-elaborate gold frames pay homage to the over-stuffed style found

aboard ocean-liners a century ago.

We take one of the lifts outside the restaurant four floors up and arrive at the Boardwalk Café on Deck 12. Besides a row of cabins with balconies, this deck and Deck 13 are devoted mainly to sporting activity. The Boardwalk offers fast food, under the open sky if desired. Decks 12 and 13 are the highest freely accessible points on board; only the funnel and mainmast are higher. The two decks boast a great deal of free area, some of which is marked out for the traditional shuffleboard, indispensable aboard a real transatlantic liner. In the roofed-over part of Deck 12 is the Pavilion Pool, which is open to passengers of all ages. Apart from the thalassotherapy Basin in the Canyon Ranch Spa Club it is the only interior pool aboard. Over the pool is the Magrodome – a glass sliding roof which can be opened in suitable weather. Golf simulators can be found on this deck. While Micky Arison wanted a viewing lounge above the bridge, Stephen Payne convinced him that on an ocean liner the bridge must be the highest point with a view ahead, for security reasons and

The Pavilion Pool is protected by a glass roof which can be opened if required

CUNARD

also by tradition. Payne made the minor concession of having the roof of Deck 13 above the bridge: behind it small platforms on both sides of the ship allow a view above the heads of the captain and officers, but they are rather ill-suited to the passenger of smaller stature.

The great, squat funnel can be seen here. Two sirens or foghorns are easily visible, fitted to a platform just above the mantle. *QE2* brought one of these, an original steam siren from the old

Fitted just above the mantle of the *QM2*'s funnel are two foghorns made by the Swedish firm Kockums. One of the horns saw service aboard the original *Queen Mary*

AUTHOR'S COLLECTION

Queen Mary, to Southampton on 18 May 2002. The horn was given to Cunard on long-term loan from the museum ship at Long Beach for installation alongside an exact replica. Directly after berthing at Southampton, the six-foot-long instrument was examined and overhauled by technicians of the manufacturer Kockums of Sweden. Lacking steam, the *QM2* sirens are operated by compressed air. This gives them a hoarser sound compared with those of the *Queen Mary*, although the 'Basso Profundo' is still impressive. The Bass A (two octaves and two notes below middle C) can be heard at up to ten sea miles.

The stairway descends two decks to where a look-out platform provides a breathtaking view ahead so long as the air stream does not roar off the forward upper works too strongly. Two glass panoramic lifts, one on each side of the ship below the bridge wing, take us to Deck 9 to terminate our tour of the ship in one of the finest rooms aboard, the Commodore Club. This cocktail bar occupies the entire breadth of the bridge front. It does not extend very far back

The elegant Commodore Club is one of the finest public rooms aboard

CUNARD

and the great panoramic windows admit daylight all day. Blue is the dominant colour – sky and sea outside, a sea-blue patterned carpet within. Along the forward part of the room are groups of four comfortable armchairs in cream leather or red-brown cushioning and small cocktail tables. In harmonious contrast the wall coverings are of warm mahogany. Facing the panoramic windows is the extended bar, its centrepiece being a large, illuminated and very

Churchill's Cigar Lounge has a bust of the cigar-smoking statesman in a niche

CUNARD

detailed model of the *QM2*. The lateral wings give the room great width, and to provide a more intimate atmosphere these areas are sectioned off by low partitions. There is a piano on the portside. Ceiling lighting in continuous bands and spotlights provide pleasant illumination.

Since the Commodore Club is a little remote from the other public rooms and shipboard night-life, in the daytime it is an oasis of tranquillity in which one is never lonely. After breakfast the first passengers arrive, book in hand maybe, to enjoy the view over the sea through the great windows, or an interesting conversation over aperitifs and cocktails. While the often loud music in the Chart Room or Golden Lion Pub may disrupt conversation, the Commodore Club is the perfect rendezvous for passengers wishing to spend a quiet evening with

a drink. Bright Persian blinds cover the windows at night, and the music is just loud enough to induce a comfortable atmosphere but not too loud for a quiet conversation.

The adjoining Churchill's Lounge, a survivor of the Smoking Lounge once to be found on every ocean giant, is part of the Commodore Club. From a nook a bust of the British statesman watches over the conversation in this rather masculine room with its cigar showcase and heavy brown and black armchairs. A glass of brandy or port can be ordered from the Commodore Club to accompany a Havana cigar.

In the baking hot summer of 2003, work continued at St-Nazaire to complete the *QM2* on schedule. The arrival of the modified Mermaid pods required Dock C to be emptied. This enabled the final coats of paint to be applied to the gigantic hull. On board workers were busily engaged in completing the internal structure. As a special measure, Cunard had insisted that to minimise the possibility of fires by short circuits, the power cables should be laid without any breaks or joints   work which could not be done by machine – and a team spent weeks passing the miles of heavy cable inch by inch into the cable shafts. It was easier for the cabin installers since the complete units were shipped aboard by cargo lift and brought by steel rollers to their predetermined locations. Every cabin was quality-controlled and checked over minutely for damage before being sealed for when Cunard would take possession of the ship.

Finally the great day arrived, and on 25 September 2003 *QM2* put to sea under her own power for four days of trials. She cast off at 1730 from Dock C towed by six tugs. 'It was great to finally take her out to the open ocean, where she belongs,' Captain Warwick stated after the trials. He was not her Master, however, for the ship remained the property of Chantiers de l'Atlantique and was under the command of a French dockyard captain and flying the French flag. The French authorities had authorised the trials under the usual conditions, particularly certain minimum requirements regarding safety on board. Three hundred fire-brigade hoses had been supplied a few days before from Germany. A couple of hours before sailing the four Mermaid pods were test-run. As *QM2* left the dock under tow and turned her bow towards the

sea, dockworkers and St-Nazaire city dwellers crammed every vantage point along the banks of the Loire. Traffic on the great suspension bridge across the river came to a standstill. Drivers simply pulled over and got out to see the ship of which the city – if not all France – was so proud. A maritime event of this magnitude, everybody agreed, had last occurred when the *France* had sailed in 1961. For the first time in thirty-six years the steam horn of the first *Queen Mary* played a duet with the replica siren to announce the imminent departure of a *Queen*.

Under a blue sky and escorted by a flotilla of yachts, motor boats, excursion vessels and five helicopters, *QM2* got under way and headed down the Loire for Biscay. For the first few hours she ran at the modest speed of twenty-two knots. On board the navigation equipment was calibrated, and then the ship's systems were

In July 2003 *QM2* was already recognisable as a near-complete ship; only her full paintwork needed to be applied

AUTHOR

25 September 2003: *Queen Mary 2* takes to sea for the first time

CUNARD

subjected to light and to progressively heavier nautical tests – dropping and weighing anchor, manoeuvring, emergency stops. In an emergency turn with rudders hard over, *QM2* inclined only 9 degrees – a fully acceptable performance.

The first speed tests served to establish degrees of vibration and to verify the data provided two and a half years before in the model tests at the Maritime Research Institute, Wageningen. Since the ship's hull had not received its final coat of anti-fouling paint, which has the dual purpose of reducing algae growth and keeping the hull surface as free of friction as possible, the final official speed trials were scheduled for the second outing in November. *QM2* reached 29.21 knots and thus the contractual top speed of 29.35 knots was easily attainable. Especially noteworthy was the acceleration rate from nought to twenty-eight knots in only seven minutes. The sensitive steam turbines of her predecessor, whose engines could only be stepped up in stages, would have required three hours for the same procedure.

The first voyage was also used as a photo opportunity from the air, and Cunard's press department was already awaiting the results. Since the first computer sketch in November 1999 the public had been supplied with more and more 'artist's impressions'; now they could see the finished ship or at least an almost complete vessel, the first stroll of 'Her Majesty' without make-up. In the sunlight the bridge front shone white. The black parts (later applied to evoke memories of the first *Queen Mary*) were still absent. In the photos one can see an improvised railing to prevent workers falling from the bridge roof. More striking was the unpainted lateral superstructure, and for publicity purposes photographs were carefully selected in which the angle and light concealed this more efficiently. Ever since, these pictures,

QM2 has three anchors, two in regular use and a third being a spare positioned on the forecastle forward of the wave-deflector. Each anchor weighs twenty-three tons. More significant, however, is the weight of the anchor chains for keeping the ship on station. At 2,500 feet they are almost double the length of the ship and they weigh 273 tons.

despite numerous batches of more recent photos, have been reproduced, often cleverly touched up to suggest a finished livery.

'Considering that *QM2* is a prototype ship, the first trials were an unqualified success, her performance exceeding all expectations,' Stephen Payne summarised on 29 September 2003 at the conclusion of the sea trials. Back in dock, work continued to meet the deadline. The shipyard was liable for expensive penalty payments if the liner could not be handed over to Cunard on 22 December 2003. And, as always with a project of this size when the 'hot phase' comes, the new Cunarder was now at the focal point of the media. As if late delivery was what they wanted to conjure forth, smaller and larger incidents made headlines – always with a doleful finger pointing to the approaching delivery date.

Of course, one is inclined to assume increasing nervousness among those with responsibilities, visualising problems which might interfere with the ship's commissioning at the last moment. The maiden voyage of *QE2* had been delayed by over six months while technical staff at the John Brown yard despaired whether the endless problems with the ship's turbines could ever be overcome. In August 2003 the press reported the possible collapse of the Alstom concern. Despite a 'lifebelt' of 3 billion euros thrown to them only eighteen months before by the EU and no fewer than thirty banks, debts had now soared to 5 billion. A not inconsiderable demand for compensation by Celebrity Cruises for the never-ending trouble with the pod-drive for the Millennium Class added to this. Cunard countered that the yard had guaranteed delivery of the ship despite these difficulties. Nevertheless, sombre tones were sounded in the preface to a special publication authored by Patrick Boissier to mark the commissioning of *QM2*, although he acknowledged his yard's merits within the Alstom group.

Slave labour was the accusation doing the

rounds in October 2003. The personnel at the French yards were organised in trade unions, but rumours hinted at subcontractors hired from outside the EU paying 'starvation wages'. Despite specific protection in contracts between yard and subcontractors, among the 700 firms involved in the construction work it was reported officially that three had received warnings, and a Romanian firm whose employees were responsible for installing the air conditioning had its contract terminated on the grounds of inadequate workmanship.

On 14 October 2003 it was announced that

Hand over ceremony luncheon

Déjeuner de cérémonie de livraison

22 décembre / december 2003

HM the Queen had accepted the invitation of the Line to name G32 at Southampton on 8 January 2004. This must have been a relief for the planners since the Queen had left it several weeks before replying. It was rumoured that Her Majesty was 'not amused' that a ship bearing her grandmother's name had been built in France. Only the Queen herself knows the truth of the matter. She only rarely accepts appointments in the month of January. In any case her acceptance was a great honour for the company and the ship.

Journalists and guests of honour who were permitted to go aboard reported indescribable chaos and a feverish pace. Those who know anything about shipbuilding understand that this is not abnormal. Outwardly well advanced towards completion, on 7 November 2003 the ship left Dock C for the second time for extensive sea trials. Cunard had hoped to run the measured mile off the Isle of Arran in the Irish Sea, where the first three Queens had completed their trials, but this was refused by the French authorities on the grounds that the ship had no classification certificate and must remain in French waters. *QM2* passed her second set of trials very successfully. Two of these tests were of special interest: an eight-hour run at full speed and the establishment of her maximum speed. This turned out to be 29.62 knots over the measured mile, although Cunard was quick to point out that the liner had exceeded thirty knots for a short while. For the last part of these tests the French yard captain handed Captain Warwick the wheel – actually more a control stick aboard *QM2* – and he later admitted how impressed he was at the new ship's manoeuvrability.

Now only a catastrophe, it seemed, could prevent the handover of *QM2* to Cunard on time, and yet the last weeks at St-Nazaire were to be overshadowed by tragedy. On Saturday 15 November 2003, Chantiers de l'Atlantique held an open day aboard *QM2* in which proud yard

The bridge of the
Queen Mary 2

CUNARD

workers could give friends and colleagues a look at their work and the shipboard luxury. For this purpose a bridge had been made to link the ship with the quayside of the empty Dry Dock C. Bridges of this kind were used daily by yard employees, but to make it easier for hundreds of visitors to go aboard, a broader bridge had been supplied. This proved to have insufficient stability to take the weight of forty-four visitors. According to eyewitnesses, at 1422 the bridge folded in its centre and its shore anchorage tore free and hit the hull, while the bridge plunged some fifty feet towards the floor of the dock. Seconds later the attachment to the ship gave way and the bridge fell on the victims below. Fifteen people were killed and twenty-eight injured, some seriously.

The enthusiastic mood of the final few weeks was destroyed. 'There has never been a similar tragedy here before,' stated Joel Batteux, Mayor of St-Nazaire. 'How could these people die at the foot of the proudest symbol of our city?' The following Monday the yard closed for the day out of respect for the victims. The investigation into the cause continued. The previous day the

French President, Jacques Chirac, visited the yard as a gesture of respect. HM the Queen sent a message stating: 'I would like to express my deepest sympathy and condolences to the families and friends of those killed in this tragedy. My thoughts and prayers are with them.' The European Parliament observed a minute's silence.

Again it was asked whether this would delay the planned delivery of the ship. Cunard hastened to give assurance that the ship would be commissioned as scheduled and the naming ceremony by the Queen would not be affected. It is always difficult to hold a major event after this kind of tragedy. How to proceed was a matter of personal conscience. In this sense it was perhaps not incorrect to proceed with the celebrations provided due respect was shown.

As was to be expected from an enterprise the size of the *QM2*, the last weeks before the handover were marked by busy and hectic work to meet the deadline. Finally, on 22 December 2003, the ship was ready to be received by its new owners. At the foot of the main (and only) mast a deputation of worthies of both undertakings assembled: Patrick Boissier, the heads of the planning staffs, Captain Ronald Warwick, Pamela Conover, Micky Arison and the watchkeeping officers of the new liner. To the sound of the 'Marseillaise' and at Boissier's command the French flag was lowered. Captain Warwick stepped forward to complete the ceremony: 'Hoist the Red Ensign!' The British national anthem rang out and the flag of the Merchant Navy rose to the masthead. *QM2* now belonged to Cunard. Earlier that day the Line had made its closing payment to the yard. She had cost €870 million to build, the most expensive passenger ship of all time – and her 148,528 gross tons made her the largest passenger ship ever until the *Freedom of the Seas* deprived her of the title in 2006. A gala dinner was then held in the Britannia Restaurant for 600 guests of honour, the first time guests had attended a reception aboard.

During the day the first luggage had been put into the holds. *QM2* would be allowed four days for the crossing to England, and not only the personal effects of the crew were stowed for the voyage, but also those of Cunard personnel who had spent several years in St-Nazaire monitoring the construction work. Stephen Payne was one of the latter. The departure from St-Nazaire next day went ahead without great ceremony: the recent tragedy at the dockyard was too fresh in the mind. It was a departure not without regrets. For four years the city had been at the centre of the growing interest around the ship. For many citizens it had been a workplace. For many months the great silhouette had been a monument dominating the city.

Now the hour of sailing – not scheduled exactly – had arrived. Every free place along the banks of the Loire was crowded with sightseers, many of them holding candles. On the suspension bridge over the Loire traffic came to a standstill. To the sound of her sirens *QM2* took leave of France, headed for the open sea and was soon beyond the horizon. Thus ended the first chapter in the life of the world's biggest ocean liner. The next, possibly more exciting, chapter was about to begin. The Cunard publicity machine had been preparing the public for the arrival of the new flagship since its conception, and now it went all out. The ship's name was on everyone's lips.

The ship herself spent Christmas in the Bay of Biscay off the coasts of France and Spain, giving the crew the opportunity over four days to find their way about and to test the ship's machinery and its technical systems in practice. As part of the familiarisation procedure, *QM2* visited Vigo and practised manoeuvring to ensure that her entry into Southampton would be flawless.

Photographers engaged by Cunard swarmed over all areas of the ship, visiting her magnificent cabins and public rooms, hundreds of yards-long corridors and great expanses of deck surface, and capturing all on film at their leisure as future publicity material for Cunard. Whenever subsequently one sees photos of the *QM2* in a Cunard brochure one can be pretty sure that these originated during this first major cruise of the ship. And finally the new Cunarder had her first great arrival: despite the rain, thousands welcomed the *QM2* to her port of registry, Southampton, on Boxing Day 2003. Whether on the Isle of Wight, along the banks of the Solent or at all vantage points which the city had to offer, everybody looked for a good spot from which to welcome the greatest passenger ship in the world. *QM2* was the star of the day.

Three fire-brigade boats preceded the liner into the Solent, pumping huge fountains of

---

It is often mentioned that when it was commissioned *QM2* was the largest and most expensive passenger ship ever. There are further superlatives which can be applied:

- With 8,500 volumes her library is the greatest afloat.
- The Queens Room is not only the greatest ballroom at sea but at forty-two by twenty-five feet in size it is the largest dance floor afloat.
- On Deck 7 is the longest jogging route at sea.
- In the history of shipbuilding no ship has ever previously had such large illuminated letters as those at the foot of the funnel.
- And the ship's hospital is the largest at sea.

water into the air. Despite the time of year and weather conditions, a large number of boats and sailing craft accompanied the great ocean liner to her berth at the Queen Elizabeth II Terminal (named after the monarch, not the ship). 'The arrival of *Queen Mary 2* is one of the most keenly anticipated events of recent years,' Mayoress Parvin Damani declared, 'She is hugely important to our economy and to Southampton's standing as a great maritime city. We are very honoured that Her Majesty has agreed to name the ship and it will be a fitting send-off for so majestic a vessel.' At the same time Cunard announced that Captain Ronald W Warwick had been promoted; Commodore Warwick was now following finally in his father's footsteps. He said that it was the finest way to round off what had already been a wonderful week.

QM2 remained at Southampton for eighteen days prior to her maiden voyage, an astronomically long period in harbour by today's standards. It was not a long lay-up, however – the ship had to be prepared and fitted for her impending career at sea, and whatever was lacking in the engine-room, crew offices, cabins, kitchens and bars was now shipped aboard. At the same time Cunard presented its new flagship to the public. It was almost impossible for 'ordinary mortals' to get aboard, but in a series of ship tours, night departures and receptions invited guests of honour were courted and the press given an overview so that the man in the street could form his own opinion of the *QM2*'s furbishings. Those wanting a closer look came alongside the hull in boats. Private yacht movements in Southampton harbour were unusually numerous for the time of year, while ferries of the Red Funnel Line to the Isle of Wight, which pass frequently every day close to the Queen Elizabeth II Terminal, reported increased passenger numbers.

Design of the Planetarium, an exterior view during construction and the finished work

DESIGNTEAM

The high point of the 'pause for breath' before the maiden voyage was undoubtedly the naming of the ship by HM the Queen on 8 January 2004. Her Majesty and Prince Philip arrived at Southampton at midday and were received for a tour of the ship by Pamela Conover. Officers and service staff paraded the Grand Lobby, the engine-room personnel were presented to the royal visitors and photos were taken, after which the royal party divided, the Queen visiting the Royal Court Theater, the Planetarium and the Library, where she signed the guest book. As a memento of her visit she received a bronze pen-holder made from a propeller of the *Queen Mary*. On her way to the bridge the Queen took the opportunity to speak to various crew members to gain their impressions of the ship. Prince Philip was given a more technically orientated tour to the engine control room, the ship's hospital, the waste disposal unit and finally the bridge, where he signed his name below that of Her Majesty.

The main event of the day began at 1530. Near the Queen Elizabeth II Terminal the Cunard Line had erected a hall some fifty feet - high whose glass front facing the water was concealed behind dark curtains. Behind it was a large stage and, towards the back of the hall, seating for 2,000 guests of honour. The city of Southampton had invested £50,000 to install a video screen in nearby Mayflower Park for the townspeople, while other screens were set up in

If she was not a media star already, *QM2* certainly become one upon commissioning

CUNARD, AUTHOR'S COLLECTION

indoor malls. After morning wind and rain the skies cleared at midday and it remained clear and cool for the ceremony. A forty-five-minute concert by the Band of the Royal Marines from Portsmouth set the scene with a rendering of maritime and patriotic melodies, ending with Edward Elgar's 'Pomp and Circumstance March No 1'. Following that the public rose and to the strains of the national anthem HM the Queen and Prince Philip came to the stage to be

welcomed by Pamela Conover. In her introduction she said:

> *Queen Mary 2* is a transatlantic liner with all the dignity and grace of the liners of the past; but she is also a transatlantic liner of the future with comforts and technology undreamt of when *Queen Elizabeth 2* was launched. Just as the original *Queen Mary* was the herald of an earlier golden age of ocean travel, so this ship heralds the new golden age; she represents no less than the triumph of a great tradition, a great British tradition of which we can all be proud.

There followed a short film, *For Queen and Country*, on the video screen in the hall showing the recent history of Cunard and ending with a representation of the Royal Mail flag on the ensign mast of *QM2*. On her transatlantic voyages the liner would always convey quantities of mail to the United States and thus had the right to the prefix RMS (Royal Mail Steamer), as did so many of her illustrious predecessors. Surprisingly, despite public appreciation of this aspect of Cunard history, it is rare for the prefix to be used. Next followed a rendering of the hit song 'Proud' by the British soul singer Heather Small, and as this finished the curtain behind the stage fell to reveal the glass frontage behind which towered the ship's enormous bow.

An impressed murmur rose in the viewing gallery, and many were brought to tears when Jim Motherwell, the court bagpipe player at Buckingham Palace, began the spiritual 'Amazing Grace', which was taken up by the soprano Lesley Garrett and the Royal Marines Band. The Bishop of Winchester, the Right Reverend Michael Scott-Joynt, then blessed the ship and in French remembered the victims of the accident at St-Nazaire in November. The ceremony reached its high point when Commodore Warwick invited the Queen to the stage to name the ship. At the lectern she proclaimed: 'I name this ship *Queen Mary Two*.

May God bless her and all who sail in her.' So saying, she pressed a button on the lectern to release a three-litre magnum of Veuve Cliquot, which smashed against the ship's side. Had the bottle remained intact this would have been a bad omen, and the precaution had been taken previously to weaken it by careful filing. The guests in the hall, Mayflower Park and the

'Ode to Joy' from Beethhoven's Ninth played by the Royal Marines Band, accompanied the pyrotechnics which dignified the ceremony

CUNARD

shopping malls clapped and cheered while the whistles of *QM2* gave three deep blasts. Commodore Warwick asked the public to join him in three cheers for Her Majesty. The band began the 'Ode to Joy' from Beethoven's Ninth and the wintry skies over Southampton were lit by a grand firework display. After the royal party left for London, a gala dinner was served in the Britannia Restaurant. Four days remained before the maiden voyage, and these were marked by gala and benefit events. 12 January 2004 arrived, and the *QM2* story began.

That morning the first passengers came aboard – the first 'pure' paying passengers who had booked the voyage in the normal manner and were not present in some capacity as guests of honour. In contrast to later arrivals they were fortunate enough, once they had unpacked their trunks, to be able to look around. Since the crew was busy with preparations for the voyage and the shipboard establishments were not yet open,

these few hours offered them time to settle in and study the Daily Programme describing the night-time entertainments, presentations, concerts and possible trips ashore along the two-week route of the voyage. At 1700 embarkation was complete. Altogether 2,519 passengers teemed on the decks and in the public rooms in excited anticipation of the departure. The *QM2* resembled a gigantic beehive.

The temperature in Southampton was a frosty four degrees centigrade, but the clear fine weather persisted. The atmosphere aboard and ashore was such that nobody minded. The Veuve Cliquot served on deck did the rest. At 1730 *QM2* cast off on her maiden voyage. She left her berth stern first to manoeuvre and stopped off Mayflower Park. On the opposite bank a majestic firework display set the scene for the new liner. Passengers waved small Union Jacks and to the mournful roar of the great foghorns *QM2* moved down the Solent, passed the Bramble Sandbanks and the Isle of Wight and entered the open sea.

Certainly to the disappointment of some passengers and to the delight of a few purists, during the first two days of the voyage the ship displayed her sea-keeping qualities in fighting a storm with hurricane gusts while heading westwards through the English Channel. A concert by the star guest Dame Shirley Bassey had to be postponed because of seasickness. Cunard was probably correct in its decision not to send the ship on a North Atlantic passage for her first voyage, even though the traditionalists would have considered it proper. Most passengers must have been grateful for the more southerly, less stormy course over the Atlantic. The schedule involved three ports of call on the eastern side of the Atlantic: after two stormy but changeable days at sea *QM2* berthed at Funchal, Madeira, on 15 January. The weather had cleared as the liner arrived in the early morning, and the passengers were entertained by what was to become a pleasant routine to these three ports

MAIDEN VOYAGE
BIENVENIDO · QUEEN MARY 2 · WELCOME
VIAJE INAUGURAL

M2

CUNARD

17 · ENERO · 2004

LAS PALMAS DE GRAN CANARIA

17ᵗʰ · JANUARY · 2004

of call: flotillas of private boats, launches and small passenger craft approached the new arrival as escorts into the harbour. Police boats kept clear the area surrounding her hull. The curious began to throng the shore for their first look at the ship, which had been headline news already for days. *QM2* was the star guest of the day, the crew as much moved by the reception as the passengers standing on the Promenade Decks or the balconies of their cabins as witnesses to the spectacle.

On the quayside Madeirans wore traditional island dress, and every passenger received a bottle of special label Madeira port. A constant stream of onlookers made the pilgrimage to the harbour all day long to see the *QM2*. The city itself seemed deserted. A similar enthusiastic reception with equally tight security measures was prepared next day by inhabitants and tourists at Santa Cruz on the island of Tenerife. The ship left Madeira at 1800, allowing the passengers the whole of the following day to reconnoitre Tenerife, visit its beaches, take an excursion or explore alone. The liner cast off from there at 2230, leave being taken to a breathtaking fireworks display ashore.

Overnight *QM2* made the short run to Las Palmas on Gran Canaria. If the reception accorded the ship on the two previous days had been enthusiastic, this one was frenetic! The passengers were greeted on the quayside like pop stars by a great multitude and almost had to fight their way to the waiting taxis. On the quay artists had created a sand-image of a bow-on view of *QM2*. Each passenger received a copy in the form of a poster, and there was a constant hustle of onlookers outside the barriers, hoping for souvenirs – particularly shipboard postcards and bar tabs with the Cunard logo which passengers distributed. That evening *QM2* took

A special welcome was prepared to greet *QM2* on her arrival at Gran Canaria

CUNARD, DIRK HEIENBROCK COLLECTION

her leave to another fireworks display arranged at five different points in sequence.

From Las Palmas the liner embarked on her four-day Atlantic crossing, giving the passengers the chance to know the ship for herself, make new acquaintances aboard, enjoy the entertainment, simply relax, take in the sea air, let mundane thoughts drift away during a walk on deck. Whereas in previous days the talk had been of going ashore, now the Daily Programme listed all the specialities and diversions of an Atlantic voyage: literary and scientific talks, some of them of a popular nature, film shows, a meeting with former *Queen Mary* passengers, lessons in bridge or how to work a computer, dance courses. Anyone who found the view of the open ocean from a deckchair too boring could find plenty to enjoy elsewhere.

The high point of every evening was dinner. The Todd English restaurant waived its surcharge for the maiden voyage, but a guest could make only a single reservation. The evenings belonged to the variety and concert offerings in the theatre, conversation to music with a drink in one of the bars or on the dance-floor in the Queens Room; an invitation to a cocktail party in the Commodore's cabin or the luxurious Officers' Wardroom for specially selected guests. The *QM2* became the stage for that kind of noisy celebration which every voyager associates with the transatlantic passage, only a little more brilliant, merrier and with rather higher-carat VIPs – after all, this was the maiden voyage.

The days at sea ended on the morning of 22 January, when *QM2* entered Bridgetown, Barbados. If the European passengers expected the red-carpet treatment of the previous calls this was a let-down, for the arrival of *QM2* was business as usual for the Barbadian population. This can be explained by the fact that while for decades Europeans considered cruises to be for the rich and famous, and too expensive even for the middle classes, in the United States there had been a mass market for cruise holidays from early on. Outside the luxury segment there was and is a large market offering comfortable but less luxurious ships with voyages every week to the Caribbean and West Indies or from the Pacific coast to Hawaii. Several large cruise ships put into Barbados daily and a new arrival is not exciting, even if she wears the Cunard livery and is called *QM2*. Therefore the Cunarder had to share an anchorage with four other large passenger ships: *European Vision*, *Costa Classica*, *Carnival Spirit* and *Seven Seas Navigator*.

Passengers aboard the *European Vision* in particular must have watched the arrival and departure of *QM2* with a certain envy. The shipowners, Festival Cruises, had gone into liquidation the previous day, and the ship was arrested at Bridgetown. Although the passengers had a roof over their heads, the cruise was over and they had to make their own way back to the

USA. After the *QM2* guests spent a day on the tropical island and its beaches, the ship left with little ceremony late that evening and arrived on the second day, 24 January 2004, at St John in the US Virgin Islands as the last intermediate stop. The quays were occupied by the cruise ships *Galaxy*, *Dawn Princess* and *Adventure of the Seas*, forcing *QM2* to anchor in the roadsteads and ship her passengers ashore in tenders, which wasted a lot of time and caused irritation. After one last day at sea came the grand finale on 26 January, when the maiden voyage ended at Fort Lauderdale, and in contrast to the Caribbean welcomes the new ocean liner was given a grand reception in Florida. Waving Union Jacks, the Stars and Stripes and Cunard flags, passengers pressed to the ship's rail as the skyline of Fort Lauderdale, probably the world's largest cruise-ship harbour, came into view. Many buildings displayed banners welcoming the ship. The usual flotilla of boats bobbed up and down ahead and astern of the liner, and the destroyer USS *Carney* and the coastguard cutter *Gannet* escorted *QM2* into harbour. The vanguard was a fire-boat sending up fountains of red, white and blue dyed water, giving foredeck passengers an unexpected shower.

Micky Arison, 'family head' of the Carnival Corporation and thus also of *QM2*, awaited the arrival of this 'youngest addition' to his great fleet on the quayside. While passengers and luggage were whisked away to hotels or airports by waiting taxis, limousines and buses, a celebration was held on the quay in which Jeb Bush, Governor of Florida, welcomed the *QM2* officially to the state. Thus ended the successful maiden voyage of *QM2*. Ship and crew had been worked up and were ready to embark on a programme of transatlantic voyages and cruises to all parts of the world.

Much to the satisfaction of company and crew, the inaugural voyage had been an unforgettable experience for all passengers, and no great problems had arisen. Cunard admitted

26 January 2004: *QM2* entering Fort Lauderdale, Florida, at the end of her maiden voyage

CUNARD

to a few technical defects, but in comparison with many other maiden voyages, that of *QM2* had been remarkably smooth. There will always be critics, and since negative headlines sell better, *QM2* came under fire. Journalists sought out the moaners and groaners among the passengers in order to find something bad to go with all the praise. Since the only inconvenience had been the failure of the hot water system for a brief period, attention was focused on the crew.

Many crew members were overworked, inexperienced and bad-tempered, it was alleged. In the Britannia Restaurant especially there had been extremely long delays in serving the courses. Next came reports about harsh working conditions with sixteen-hour shifts and poor pay. For this reason ninety crew members were supposed to have resigned and left the ship within the first six weeks. Cunard replied that the true figure was five, not a high percentage and within normal limits for a crew of 1,258. Another headline at the same time must have made mindful observers smile about some journalists' sense of reality: alledgedly

Menu card for the tandem transatlantic crossing

CUNARD, DIRK HEIENBROCK COLLECTION

Buckingham Palace was concerned at the turnover of service staff who left the Royal Court to find better pay aboard the *QM2*.

Sixteen-hour working days are excessive, but not unusual in cruise ships, and a ship such as *QM2* has little space for off-duty staff. There is a crew pub, the Pig and Whistle, a swimming pool and a fitness room, but that is it for weeks on end of eight hours' sleep and eight hours off-duty. Therefore many crew members prefer a long working day, make the best of every working hour and look forward all the more to long periods of shore leave. By European standards the pay is certainly not extraordinary. That is the reason why most stewards on cruise ships are Filipinos, for whom the pay is very healthy by their islands' standards. Apart from satisfying shareholders and associates, the outgoings of a shipping company have a direct relationship to voyage cost. Bankruptcies among recently founded cruise companies of recent years prove that though the business can be lucrative, the ground can crumble as a result of a number of imponderables.

Whatever the case with the *QM2* crew, they were still in the familiarisation phase during the maiden voyage and an ocean liner is complex. But even so there were still occasional reports of poor service in the Britannia Restaurant even two years later, and one can only assume that the restaurant, with 1,300 guests per sitting and two sittings per evening, was overwhelmed by the sheer scale. Loyal Cunard passengers also complained during the first year that in contrast to *QE2*, the new liner had suffered a certain misalignment, for example that the dress rules prescribed only two formal evenings with ballgown and tuxedo on the six-day Atlantic crossings as opposed to the four previously (for the first and last evenings at sea more casual attire is permitted). Evil tongues maintained that Cunard feared it could not fill the ship with passengers 'of the right class' and that the 'proletariat' was now wheedling its way in. Once before, when *QE2* had entered service in 1969, an attempt had been made to cut back on the transatlantic traditions, but this had not been well received. Cunard now hastened to offer its clientele what they expected from the time-honoured shipping line, and stricter rules for formal dress aboard *QM2* were soon imposed. Criticism circulating in the public rooms was based on individual taste. While some considered the prescribed elegance to be too

Captain Ronald Warwick was Master of *QE2* for thirteen years before assuming command of *QM2*. Previously he had spent many years on Cunard's earlier liners. When asked by journalists what ship he preferred he would usually answer with a smile: 'Do you dance with one lady when you are crazy to be with another?'

conservative, others complained that inwardly the *QM2* resembled the show lounge of a Las Vegas hotel. These negative points were voiced by the few: for many thousands of travellers a voyage on the *QM2* was an unforgettable experience.

One of the few weak points, especially for ocean-liner enthusiasts, was the Maritime Quest. Since its introduction aboard *QE2* in 1994, the Heritage Trail, a circular tour peppered with Cunard memorabilia, had given passengers great pleasure. Cunard wanted to offer the guests of *QM2* the same experience and so during the construction of the ship a London firm, the Open Agency, had been commissioned to design some large panels to that effect. These were placed at various points, particularly along the corridors between the public rooms, and portrayed the history of Cunard by means of a mixture of historic pictures and photographs. This gave passengers *en passant* the opportunity to learn something of the history of Cunard and its ships. At the Purser's Desk one could hire equipment for an audio tour for more information. While basically a good idea, the panels came in for criticism on the grounds that their colourful aggressive presentation rather reminded one of the front page of a tabloid newspaper and was certainly not appropriate to

the ambience of an ocean giant. Others considered the information too scanty, a doubtful objection since the library is rich in maritime literature. Enthusiasts thought the actual quality of the information inadequate and, having identified numerous errors in the history, wondered why the material had not been read over by an historian with knowledge of Cunard history. Enthusiasts also complained that whereas the *QE2* was richly endowed with authentic historical pieces, apart from oil paintings the new ship did not have original items on show.

Compared with the overall result, these were minor complaints, and although *QM2* was never long out of the headlines, these were rarely adverse. Apart from the notorious 'whingers' the bulk of passengers were impressed by their voyage. The Nautical Institute of London declared *QM2* 'Ship of the Year', and Commodore Warwick 'Master of the Year', while the Post Office brought out a stamp featuring the ship as its design. The publicity strategists at Carnival Corporation knew how to set the scene for a ship and create worldwide interest in her, and not all opportunities to put the *QM2* into the spotlight had yet been exhausted. The next act of the Grand Première was the introduction of *QM2* to the North Atlantic service for which she had been built.

After several Caribbean voyages and an excursion to Rio for the carnival, the liner returned to Southampton on 16 April 2004 to sail the same day on her first North Atlantic crossing. Apart from the lack of a fireworks display the enthusiasm of the masses was equal to that shown for the inaugural voyage. A huge crowd of well-wishers ashore and an honour guard of some small harbour vessels saw her off. Another parallel to the maiden sailing occurred in the Atlantic when the ship proved she was the transatlantic liner Stephen Payne had designed her to be. Forced to reduce speed in a Force 10 storm, she made up for lost time once it abated.

Two Queens in Manhattan in 1948 and 2004

RINGO VARISCO, CUNARD

Some crockery was reported smashed. That her reception in New York on 22 April was accompanied by all the pomp to be expected goes without saying, but New York City's stringent security regulations obliged yachts and other private boats to stay clear of the liner, and even the Staten Island ferries had to make a detour. *QM2* was escorted by a fire-boat, several tugs, two coastguard ships and several police boats to her berth at Pier 92, where she remained the centre of attention over the next few days of gala events.

On 25 April *QE2* arrived in New York and moored near her larger sister at Pier 90. It was the first meeting of the two Cunard Queens and the first time since 1966 that two Queens had been in Manhattan together. Official press reports even asserted that it was the first time since March 1940, pointing to the lay-up there of the two older Queens early in the war, but in fact *Queen Mary* and *Queen Elizabeth* had crossed the Atlantic side by side after the great strike of merchant navy seamen in Britain in 1966.

An historic moment for the Cunard Line: *QE2* and *QM2* leave New York side by side

CUNARD

At 1930 the same day, *QM2* cast off and moved to the southern point of Manhattan to await *QE2*, whose refuelling was taking longer than planned, but finally the two ships met off the Statue of Liberty. A fireworks display lit the heavens and the two transatlantic liners headed side by side for Britain. It was a voyage long advertised and left passengers tossing up as to which ship to choose – except for the lucky one who sailed to Southampton aboard *QE2* and trans-shipped the same day to *QM2* for the return to New York. Irrespective of the ship chosen, however, it was a memorable voyage peppered with many small extras for devotees of the Queens. Throughout the crossing by day the two liners kept a mile apart, Commodore Warwick of *QM2* and Captain Ian McNaught of *QE2* operating a changeover roster in which first one and then the other led, thus providing wonderful photographic opportunities. At night a separation of two miles was maintained. The pair, led by *QE2*, arrived at Southampton on 1 May 2004 to an enormous welcome, *QE2*

making fast in the Western Docks, principally a freight terminal used occasionally for cruise ships. The new Cunarder moored at the Queen Elizabeth II Terminal.

In a ceremony aboard *QE2* Captain McNaught handed the silver trophy, which Samuel Cunard had received at Boston after the first voyage of RMS *Britannia*, into the keeping of Commodore Warwick, and thus *QM2* became the official flagship of the line. In conclusion the entertainer Sir Jimmy Savile proposed a toast to the *QE2*, which had made her first transatlantic crossing on 2 May thirty-

During the Olympic Games in Athens, *QM2* served as a hotel ship. Passengers could book outward and return voyages

CUNARD, DIRK HEIENBROCK COLLECTION

five years previously. At midday, with an honour guard of fire-brigade boats and numerous yachts, *QE2* left Southampton to an exchange of foghorn salutes and headed for Lloyd Werft, Bremerhaven, for a refit. For the *QE2* an era had come to an end. She had carried the Cunard flag on the transatlantic service for thirty-five years. For three decades she had been the only ship of her kind on the regular liner service over the classic route. This function would now be

undertaken by *QM2*. After her overhaul *QE2* retired to Southampton, from where henceforth she would be used exclusively as a cruise ship. She would cross the Atlantic only if it was a stage of a pleasure cruise – and once yearly as part of her world voyage. The *QE2* had thus become a 'pleasure steamer', but her popularity would not fade. 2003 was marketed as her 'last waltz over the Atlantic', and many of her devotees availed themselves of the opportunity. In her new role *QE2* shared the first year with *Caronia*, whose days with Cunard after twenty years were numbered: on 30 May 2003 Cunard announced an agreement with Saga Cruises whereby at the end of the 2004 season *Caronia* would pass to the cruise company to join her sister ship *Saga Rose* ex-*Sagafjord*.

The former *Vistafjord* thus began her third career in thirty-one years. After taking possession, Saga Cruises gave the ship a thorough overhaul. The entire outer skin was sandblasted and repainted, and the inner rooms refurbished to the tastes and needs of the over-fifties. When the ship left the yard in 2005 under the name *Saga Ruby* she looked brand-new with pleasing classical lines.

Before *QM2* had been commissioned, Cunard had made known that during the Olympic Games in Athens she would interrupt her normal programme for two and a half weeks for use as a hotel ship. This was a surprise since it meant a change to the published schedule for the opening year, although such a charter was bound to be financially rewarding for Cunard, and good publicity for the ship. The assembly of the cruise ships *AIDAaura, Olympia Countess* ex *Cunard Countess, Olympia Voyager, Olympia Explorer, Rotterdam* and *Oosterdam* made an impressive picture at Piraeus, Athens's port.

Whatever negative headlines had been written about *QM2* at the outset of her career, she needed little time to convince everybody to the contrary and build a following. VIPs worldwide soon flocked to sail on the new Cunarder,

November 2005: *QM2* at Blohm + Voss, Hamburg, for a first refit

THYSSENKRUPP MARINE SYSTEMS

among others Prince Mubarak of Kuwait, the comedy star John Cleese, the rock singer Rod Stewart and actors such as Richard Dreyfuss, Carrie Fisher and Jayne Seymour. The list of those who visited but did not sail is also long. A very special passenger in July 2005 who crossed the Atlantic aboard the world's greatest ocean liner instead of on a broomstick was Harry Potter. The first copy of the US edition of Joanne K Rowling's newest novel on the adventures of the student of magic, *Harry Potter and the Half-Blood Prince,* was signed by the author in Scotland, after which an employee of the publisher brought it to Southampton in the greatest secrecy. The book was put into an enormous old-fashioned sea trunk and shipped

aboard *QM2*, where it was subject to a strict security watch during the voyage.

For thirty-six years, four months and two days, the *Scythia* of 19,730 gross tons, commissioned in 1921, sailed the seas for Cunard. In 1958 she was scrapped at Inverkeithing. For many years she held the record as the longest-serving Cunarder, the famous *Aquitania*, which sailed from 1914 to 1949, running second. In the rankings the two ships were eclipsed into second and third place respectively on 4 September 2005 when *QE2* claimed the title. Despite 5.3 million sea miles 'on the clock' (further than any ship had ever sailed) the *QE2* appeared more elegant than ever before and was still some time away from her

QM2 **in swathes of morning mist in the Elbe**

STEFAN BEHN

retirement. Rumours to the contrary were denied vehemently by Cunard. All the more remarkable is her achievement when it is recalled that the many critics of the *QE2* predicted at her commissioning that the liner would be mothballed within six months.

On 7 November 2005 Cunard announced the appointment of a new President and Managing Director. Carol Marlow, a British national, is an honours graduate in Business Studies of the University of Southampton and had followed a career subsequently in tourism and tourist media. In 1997 she joined P&O and in her first assignment worked as Managing Director of the subsidiary Swan Hellenic, which was wound up in 2007.

P&O Princess Cruises (a sector of the undertaking through the acquisition of Princess Cruises by P&O) was detached from the principal company in 2000. A few years later the then No 3 in the world cruise-ship market began negotiations with the No 2, Carnival's arch-rival Royal Caribbean Cruise Lines (RCCL). A merger of the two cruise giants would have created the world's biggest cruise-ship company and relegated Carnival into second place. After long and tough bargaining, P&O Princess plc shareholders voted in April 2003 to merge with Carnival instead of RCCL. The British company then changed its name to Carnival plc and an unusual arrangement ensued: a dual-listed company, Carnival Corporation & plc, with registered head offices in Miami and London, its shares quoted simultaneously on the London and New York stock exchanges.

The restructuring of the principal company caused changes at Cunard. The connection between Cunard and the Seaborn Cruise Line had proved impractical and was dissolved. On 1 January 2005 Cunard Line was incorporated as an individual entity into the Carnival Corporation. In the wake of these changes the remnants of the once-British company were subordinated to the new subsidiary Princess Cruises, and Santa Clarita in California became Cunard's new head office. The former Managing Director of Cunard, Pamela Conover, became Chairwoman of Seaborn Cruise Line. Cunard was managed by P&O Princess Chairman Peter Ratcliffe until Carol Marlow took over from him. In the hash of firms and brands within the Carnival Corporation she had served previously as Cunard's Managing Director for Europe, Asia and Africa.

Meanwhile it had been two years since *QM2* had run her trials on the open sea and the time had come for a thorough inspection and routine overhaul of all components subject to stress, such as the main engines, the four Mermaid pods, the bow thrusters, stabilisers and suchlike. As there was no adequately large dockyard available in Britain, Cunard awarded the contract to the already well-proven German yard of Blohm + Voss, Hamburg. A sum of tens of millions was mentioned.

On the evening of 8 November 2005 *QM2* headed for the Elbe for the third time in her

short career (see Chapter 5), and although she had no passengers or itinerary she was welcomed by a loyal following of thousands of fans, who crowded thickly along the river banks, at the Hamburg fish market and on the landing quays to welcome the (then) largest passenger ship in the world. This was mainly the doing of the

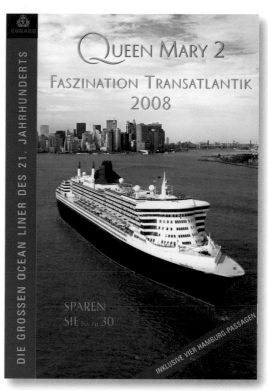

media, which had made a great song and dance about the Cunarder's arrival, an event coinciding with the presence in Hamburg of the world's largest passenger airliner, the Airbus A380. The docking planned for that evening was called off after southerly winds forced water out of the Elbe into the North Sea so that high tide at Hamburg was 30 inches below that expected, insufficient to float *QM2* safely into Blohm + Voss Dock 17. Captain Bernard Warner, relieving Commodore Warwick on this voyage, decided against going into dock until next morning on the following high tide. Once she was inside, dock employees set to work with a will, enabling Blohm + Voss to complete the contract on time. *QM2* sailed early on 19

In 2005 *QE2* celebrated the longest period in service of a Cunard liner. The company has supplied the following additional information: In her career *QE2* completed 1,383 voyages at an average speed of 24.75 knots and carried almost 3 million passengers. With the use of the Arabic '2' in her name, she has probably the most frequently misspelled ship's name in the world. No other merchant vessel has such a powerful engine-room. In the course of her thirty-six years in service *QE2* visited New York 705 times as opposed to 'only' 651 visits to Southampton. The *QE2* is the world's greatest single consumer of caviare. Since 1969 Cunard has invested fifteen times the original building cost in modernising and renovating the ship.

November for Southampton as planned.

If Cunard could have foreseen what was to befall *QM2* in 2006, they would have postponed this routine maintenance to the unscheduled dockyard visit that was imminent. The drama began on 17 January, the third day of a voyage from New York to Rio. When leaving Fort Lauderdale a jolt was reported, the bridge systems indicating a malfunction in one of the Mermaid pods. Since this was a static pod, manoeuvrability was not affected and Commodore Warwick decided to continue with the voyage. Unfortunately he was obliged to report to the US Coastguard that *QM2* had struck an underwater obstruction in the narrow harbour entrance, and the coastguard ordered the ship back for an assessment of the damage. Divers reported subsequently that damage was limited to the pod.

On 19 January the liner resumed the cruise. With only three pods her top speed was reduced although she answered the helm as normal. To their outrage, passengers had been forced to remain aboard, since landing was not permitted by the US immigration regulations, and now they learned that the intermediate stops at the Caribbean islands of St Kitts and St Lucia, and at Salvador de Bahía in Brazil, had been cancelled so that *QM2* could arrive in Rio on time.

Cunard offered the passengers a 50 per cent refund. Whereas this would certainly have been acceptable to some, and many passengers reported on the efforts of staff to provide the best holiday possible, there was discontent. A large contingent of passengers considered the

Even though she arrived only for the purpose of entering the shipyard, QM2 became the star of the annual celebrations to mark the founding of the port of Hamburg. In the foreground is one of the 'blue goals' erected throughout Hamburg in connection with the 2006 Football World Cup

THYSSENKRUPP MARINE SYSTEMS

rebate derisory and demanded a full refund. In a
conference held in the Royal Court Theater,
Commodore Warwick attempted to pour oil on
troubled waters, but e-mails had gone out from
passengers to the press, and before the ship
reached Rio, Cunard had given in and agreed to
a full refund of the voyage and flight costs. Apart
from the notorious few who never can be

placated, the situation was accepted. The
spontaneous visit of the Cunard President Carol
Marlow aboard *QM2* at Rio, to apologise on
behalf of the company for the inconvenience,
was well received.

Even on only three Mermaid pods, *QM2*
could make twenty-five knots, which was fast
enough for the remainder of her programme

once she had undergone the necessary repairs. From Rio the liner headed south around Cape Horn, becoming the largest passenger ship ever to do so, a record she will probably hold for many years. The winds and seas off the tip of South America are much feared, and the area may be the world's largest graveyard of ships. Passenger vessels usually choose the Panama

Canal to pass from Atlantic to Pacific, and even the modern 'post-Panamax' cruise ships, which are too large to transit the canal before work to widen it is complete, prefer the Cape of Good Hope. *QM2* completed the run with only three propellers and sailed northwards along the west coast of the Americas to an ecstatic welcome from 800 boats, three airships and 6,000 onlookers at Long Beach on 23 February 2006. This was the first meeting of *QM2* with her namesake *Queen Mary*, and the two Cunarders not only made an impressive picture but provided an interesting study in the development of the ocean liner since 1936. The two ships exchanged salutes by foghorn before *QM2* continued her voyage to Los Angeles.

After this visit to the Pacific side of the United States the liner retraced her path to New York, where on 15 April 2006 she ended a long tradition by being the first *Queen* since the 1930s not to use the passenger terminal at Manhattan. Its three 1,000-foot-long piers jutting out into the Hudson River had been built to serve the first two Queens, *Normandie*, *Bremen* and *Europa*, which had been too long for the old quays. After the eclipse of the Atlantic liner service the rows of piers had become superfluous and in the 1970s only the three largest had been renovated for future use by cruise ships. In the trend for pleasure cruising, the companies preferred the warmer ports of Florida, and from the mid-1980s there were no regular cruise-ship sailings from Manhattan, so that the three piers of the Manhattan cruise terminal often had a rather desolate look about them. The number of departures from New York then rose with the worldwide cruise boom, and in 2005 Norwegian Cruise Line based its ships *Norwegian Spirit* and *Norwegian Dawn* in Manhattan, where more than a million passengers now use the venerable old piers annually. These had their limitations in that they were 130 feet too short for the *QM2*, whose stern therefore projected into the Hudson. As a

When one compares these photographs of the bridge in 2005 and 2007, the enlargement of the bridge wings is obvious

THORBEN KOCKS, AUTHOR'S COLLECTION

rule no more than four ships could use the six berths because the basin between the piers was not wide enough.

The coastal watch complained at the situation: the city planners frowned. Up to 16,000 passengers frequented the terminal on the days when all berths were occupied – a substantial disruption for traffic around the harbour – to which was added a large number of supply lorries for the ships. Once the major shipping companies began to seek alternatives, Carnival came to an arrangement with the City of New York in which a berth in the Red Hook district of Brooklyn would be enlarged to include a terminal building and other infrastructure for *QM2* in consideration of a guaranteed minimum number of calls annually. The development involved a major restructuring of the former industrial area near the harbour. The terminal was inaugurated by the arrival of

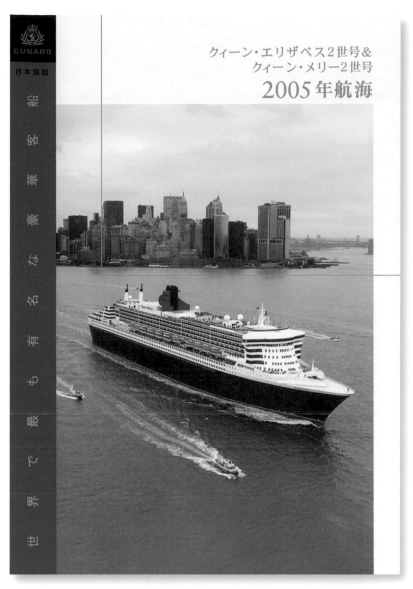

クィーン・エリザベス2世号＆
クィーン・メリー2世号
2005年航海

carnival along the waterfront. For the planners the arrival of *QM2* was naturally a bonus which promised a large increase in attendance. Her arrival that day had the additional advantage of costing nothing. The elation was soon overshadowed by the realisation that the liner's docking manoeuvre would interfere with the carnival: along the landing stages full-rigged sailing ships were moored which were the guests of the city for the occasion, and the floating pontoons were frequented by thousands of visitors. In order to get *QM2* into Dock 17, every inch of the harbour up to the landing stages was needed. These would have to be sealed off by the police for security reasons – no easy task with large crowds of sightseers. Moreover the manoeuvre had to coincide precisely with high tide. On 6 May this would be at 2300, the time when a spectacular fireworks display was scheduled. The big question was – would *QM2* get in this time at the first attempt?

The organisation and manoeuvre went off without a hitch, the ship docked as planned and 1.5 million visitors celebrated the anniversary, in which the visit of the flagship was the high point. The damaged Mermaid pod was lifted out by crane and seventy-seven hours later *QM2* was heading for the sea to begin her summer season propelled by only three pods. In November 2006 the liner docked again at Blohm + Voss for the repaired pod to be remounted, the opportunity being taken to extend each bridge wing by 6.5 feet to improve vision astern.

The merging of Cunard with Princess Cruise Line by the Carnival Corporation now made itself felt with an intermixing of staff. The thinking behind this was that the two companies could learn from each other in service and ship command structure. Employees of Princess Cruises would teach their British counterparts in the latter regard while Cunard would be the example in service standards. This basically good idea was not received positively by everyone. In

QM2 on 15 April 2006. A further survey of the damage to the Mermaid pod had shown that a repair would not be possible while the ship was on her berth, and two shipyard visits would be necessary, between which *QM2* would sail using only three pods. Blohm + Voss won the lucrative repair contract.

Late in the evening of 6 May 2006 *QM2* went into Dock 17 for her second visit to the Blohm + Voss yard. This coincided with the 817th anniversary of the founding of the port of Hamburg; since 1989 this celebration had been an annual event involving a review of ships and a

Cunard's advance into the
twenty-first century:
Queen Mary 2

CUNARD

the summer of 2006 traditionalists complained that in practice Cunard no longer existed as an entity, and aboard *QM2* there was only a single 'pure' Cunard officer, although the company continued to boast of its long history. The crews also felt a certain disquiet about the wrenching asunder of proven teams 'on orders from above'.

Since *QM2* was commissioned, Captain Paul Wright had acted as deputy to Commodore Warwick when he was absent on leave or attending training courses. In June 2005 Wright was transferred to the *Diamond Princess*. At 115,875 gross tons this was an impressive cruise ship but her image was in an entirely different league from the Cunard flagship. He was said to have been utterly crestfallen. Captain Christopher Rynd, who had previously commanded *Sapphire Princess*, was appointed his successor. Rynd was an officer who had served aboard P&O ships such as *Oronsay* and *Oriana* in 1960 and the *Uganda* before transferring to the Princess Cruises branch of the business.

One year later *QM2* underwent another major change when, after thirty-six years' service with Cunard, Commodore Ronald W Warwick 'swallowed the anchor' and was pensioned off. Cunard's PR department under Carnival's management was adept at making publicity of any event major or minor – a must in the modern world if one is to be noticed among the overflow of information – and thus Warwick went into retirement as a Cunard legend. In his thirty-six years with Cunard he had seen many changes, and had done more than anyone else to give the company a human face over the latter years. With his personal interest in the history of the ocean liner, Warwick had gone at the task wholeheartedly. To most passengers he was the picture-book image of the captain of the

proudest ocean giant. His last voyage as Master of *QM2* ended on 30 July 2006 at Southampton after an Atlantic crossing. Carol Marlow attended his departure from active duty. After an emotional hour of partying, Commodore Warwick and his wife Kim were taken by helicopter from the *QM2* upper deck to their home in Somerset.

Warwick's successor was not Christopher Rynd, who remained as captain's relief, but Captain Bernard Warner, transferred in by Cunard from Princess Cruises. For Warner it had been a simple telephone call from management: presumably it was one which gave him great pleasure. Not every day is one awarded command of a ship such as the *QM2*! In earlier years Warner had toyed with the idea of a position with Cunard, but began service with P&O in 1965 because it appeared to present better career opportunities. After service aboard freighters he joined *Oriana* in 1969 and climbed the career ladder with *Iberia*, *Canberra* and *Uganda*. He received his first command, *Island Princess*, in 1994. Continuing its custom, on 8 January 2007 Cunard promoted Warner to Commodore at the beginning of the *QM2*'s world voyage.

The liner was entering her fourth year in commission and relatively speaking was still young in service. She had her critics but most passengers left the ship at the end of a voyage with a feeling of contentment. These passengers and her devotees hope that *QM2* will complete her life span of forty years and become an icon with a long, varied and successful career, as did her predecessors. She has the ability to do so and one looks forward to what history will have to say about this first ocean liner of the twenty-first century when her time is up.

CHAPTER

4

Sailing day usually finds
the full comlement of
passengers on deck

MARTIN GRANT

GETTING
THERE
IS
HALF
THE
FUN

'What binds the clientele of today to Cunard?' That was the question that the New Yorker Deborah Natansohn asked herself when in November 2000 she took up her duties with Great Britain's former primary shipping company, now operated by the American cruise-ship giant Carnival Corporation. Alongside the 'co-branding' aspects already mentioned, she was responsible for determining Cunard's new direction, and especially for publicising *QM2* as a product. If one asked the man in the street what he associated with the name Cunard, he would probably mention some famous ship names and perhaps art deco, service with attention to detail, an ultra-British image, the great age of ocean giants. On reflection he might add 'the good old days' and think of his parents' or grandparents' generation. A glance at Cunard prospectuses of recent years seems to confirm these associations. Especially in those from the end of the twentieth century, when Cunard became a Carnival

Corporation trademark, one sees it written in elegant terms that to voyage with Cunard is to relive the Golden Age at Sea. The mixture of contemporary photographs and reproductions from historical brochures leaves no doubt that the marketing strategists – and the target clientele – of this Golden Age aim at somewhere in the 1920s and 1930s, perhaps with a few loans from the 1950s.

What was the attraction of an ocean liner of that era? Cabins with bathroom were rare even in First Class. There was no air-conditioning. The funnels emitted enough smoke and soot to make expensive dry cleaning of clothing necessary. Even if the cuisine aboard classic ships such as *Normandie* and *Île de France* remains legendary to this day, it is doubtful whether it would satisfy the modern passenger accustomed to modern dishes, stiffened with flavouring. The *Queen Mary*, before two sets of stabilisers were fitted in 1958, rolled to such an extent even in moderate seas that she inspired the author Paul Gallico to write his best-seller *The Poseidon Adventure*, subsequently made into several films, and similarly the ship in Wolfgang Petersen's 2006 film is based on the *QM2* (which is a much more stable sea-keeper). Undoubtedly one could continue this list of weaknesses of the classic ocean giant *ad infinitum*, but it would serve no purpose. In their time, most of these ships were outstanding constructions which not only satisfied all expectations, but often exceeded them. That they would eventually be overtaken by time is in

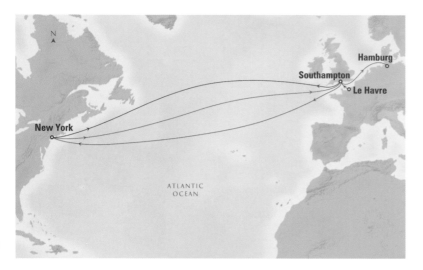

The North Atlantic routes and Cunard's main passenger ports

CUNARD

Cruise terminal or aircraft hangar? Inside the Queen Elizabeth II Terminal at Southampton

ROLF SCHWERDTNER

At home aboard

CUNARD

the nature of things. If one sees how the large passenger ferries of Europe have developed, it is clear how much the character of what is offered aboard, and the expectations of passengers, have changed over less than twenty years.

A shipping company's potential clients may begin to dream of the 'good old days' at the mention of its name. It is a fact of psychology that pleasant memories tend to outlive bad experiences. Especially for the generation which lived in the era of the transatlantic liner, there is a nostalgia for the epoch when 'somehow everything was better'. If one considers that the 'Golden Age' of the ocean giant occurred two decades before the Second World War, then one can see the dilemma confronting the Cunard marketing strategists, for the generation which can recall that time is gradually dying out. It was therefore Deborah Natansohn's job to win over as new clients the

'baby boom' generation, those born after the war and into the 1960s, for why should the 'good old days' not be those of one's parents or grandparents? These were easier to recall. However, it was not so simple as that. Behind Natansohn's thinking were psychoanalytical and marketing considerations, particularly the trend in recent years towards high-value products as against the 'luxury is greed' philosophy, and the hectic nature of life for the working population in the Internet age. There is a surplus of information; e-mails and mobile phones make man a slave to technology – and also to his employer. The dividing line between home and the workplace is becoming more blurred. Additionally there is 'free-time stress', a concept unknown a few years previously. Time has become a luxury in short supply. All this was precisely the thinking behind the new marketing strategy for Cunard voyages.

The moorings have been cast off. A stretch of blissful sea miles lies ahead

HAMISCHA DÖRING

While elsewhere shipping companies promised day-long partying, surf simulators and wall-scaling on board 'fun ships', the luxury horse in the Cunard stable offered its guests one thing above everything: time, and with it such things as rest, remoteness at sea and the feeling of not having to bother about anything and being able to spend all day doing just what one wanted – even if that be total idleness. Let us therefore experience a voyage aboard the *QM2* from Southampton to New York. The Boat Train – the express train from London's Waterloo Station to the Ocean Terminal at Southampton – has long vanished into history. But there are still trains from Waterloo to Southampton Central. After leaving the train one takes a taxi or the Cunard shuttle-bus the short distance to the Queen Elizabeth II

Terminal. One may alternatively arrive in one's chauffeur-driven limousine, but all pass through the same gate into the heavily monitored harbour area, and a few minutes later into a building resembling an aircraft hangar, behind which the great liner lies. The interior of the hall recalls little of the majesty of luxury liners of yore with bouquets of roses and emotional goodbyes. Tour coaches discharge a colourful mixture of holidaymakers, who wait patiently in a long queue stretching from the departure hall to the arrival hall. A few by their appearance and transport are clearly not of the *hoi polloi*. We line up and wait patiently, fill out a questionnaire on our health and wonder what percentage of visitors is rejected by the US authorities on health grounds.

At the desk we produce our documents, pose for digital photographs and a little later receive a plastic card bearing a photo and bar code which will serve as a credit card aboard. On a cruise it serves as the re-boarding pass. This is not a cruise, however, but a crossing; our ship has a destination, and not a little sightseeing before returning to the port of departure. Again we wait. The colourful card in our hand allocates us to one of the groups which will gradually stream to the ship. We sit in the terminal waiting room and look over our fellow-travellers. Soon our colour is called and we make our way to the waterside exit doors. A photograph is taken of each passenger against a lifebelt. We cross our fingers and hope we shall not need it. We go aboard through an airport-like boarding passage. We are on the *QM2* at last, but lose the moment in our growing excitement at the coming departure, and like a giant vacuum cleaner the liner sucks us in.

The Grand Lobby is a bustle of passengers, stewards and luggage. A representative of Cunard wearing white gloves takes our bags and leads us to our cabin through a sequence of corridors and lifts which later we cannot remember. The cabin door closes and peace

The ship's track on the ocean

AUTHOR

returns. For a moment the sudden silence surprises us; then we look around the cabin. They are roomy, these standard cabins, with or without balcony. Tasteful but not overly so. The honey-coloured suite and cream walls stand in pleasant contrast to the black trim and coverings of the furniture. A bright red sofa and matching pillows on the bed add a touch of colour. The carpet is pleasantly soft, the textiles expensive. On the bed a rubber mat has been spread out for our cases. The bathroom is not large but beautifully clean, and nothing looks cheap. The wardrobes offer plentiful space. We are anxious to unpack but our sea trunk has not yet been brought. What next? Open the gift bottle of champagne and drink to the voyage? Glance through the Daily Programme left on the small writing and dressing table? Or begin our

exploration of the ship forthwith?

An announcement relieves us of the decision. Before sailing, passengers are required to 'muster'. Holding our life-jackets we assemble at a prearranged station, where we are counted and instructed on how to act in an emergency – rather like on an aircraft. This is one of the few obligatory requirements aboard an ocean liner. Having removed our life-jackets we await the high point of departure. A party is already in full swing on the after-deck. Loud music from a live band can be heard on the quayside below. Crew members encourage passengers to participate in a polonaise. Other guests stand at the ship's rail, champagne glass in hand, looking over the roofs of the city at eye level or below the decks. Those in more reflective mood sit in deckchairs on the Promenade Deck or the Sports Deck, Deck 13, or drift between the two sides of the ship to watch the land recede. Those who prefer more solitude may enjoy the moment from their balconies. Three-quarters of the ship's cabins have one, although obviously they tend to be used more often in more southerly zones than in the raw North Atlantic.

Dockworkers below release the heavy mooring warps from the quayside bollards; the lines splash into the water before being hauled inboard. From the funnel the two foghorns blast out a mournful salute to the home city, and with a massive whirl of water the great sides of the ship move away from the quay. The voyage has begun! Those looking to see the tugs come by to assist are disappointed, for the *QM2* has no need of them. Using only bow thrusters and pods hard over at the stern, the Commodore and harbour pilot handle the departure manoeuvres. Imperceptibly the gap between ship and shore widens, slowly and then ever quicker. Below the

ship the Mermaid pods are turned to move the ship ahead – and now she will be continuously under way until the morning of the seventh day, when she arrives in New York. Just briefly we drop revolutions while transferring the pilot before reaching the open sea.

Southampton recedes. The *QM2* sails majestically down the Solent, the Hampshire shoreline to starboard. The liner enthusiast can roll off his tongue the names of all the great ships which have made this run before us. After enjoying the landscape for a while we return to our cabin. The ship awaits us, and she will be our home for five full days and six nights. We find our sea trunk in the cabin and now have the chance to brush off the dust of the journey and change our clothes. As if the Line wished to spare the new arrivals a problem with the question of dress on the first evening, it is traditional that the dress code on the first and last evenings is casual. Of the three levels of

For many it is the fulfilment of a dream: crossing the Atlantic aboard *QM2*

CUNARD

Two flags marking the ports of departure and destination, placed on the central steering module on the bridge of *QM2*, symbolise the passage for a model of the first *Queen Mary*. Each officer of the watch moves the model five and a half inches forward at the beginning of his shift so that it will complete its 'voyage' to coincide with the 'big sister'

AUTHOR

prescribed dress this is the lowest, the only prohibition being on short trousers in the restaurants. The other two stages are informal and formal. How casual is casual? Even on the first evening certain clothing is frowned upon. The customer is not king, especially not aboard *Queen Mary 2*. Could one turn out in a ragged T-shirt and old jeans? Wearing a blouse or a shirt and tie, we do not feel overdressed. Probably the answer lies somewhere between the two. One can look elegant in casual clothing, but not in one's gardening clothes.

The first evening hardly remains in the passenger's memory. People get to know each other aboard the ship. Attendance at the programme of shows is rather scanty and a number of institutions limit their productions, since passengers are busy unpacking or just wandering around the ship. In particular people who work and are at the end of a stressful week, or those who have made a long journey by public transport to reach Southampton, may

prefer to retire early. The real enjoyment will begin in the morning. Wherever one looks there is nothing but blue sky and sea. 'I am aboard *QM2*' is the first thought upon awakening for most before turning to the bedside telephone to order morning tea to be brought to the cabin. One browses the Daily Programme, delivered to the cabin the previous night, or the shipboard edition of *The Times*. Oh! Breakfast is not served in the Britannia Restaurant after 0930!

Preferring not to appear at table in a dressing gown with hair uncombed, we decide to skip formal breakfast this morning and use the King's Court instead, which remains open until 1100. We discover to our dismay that the same idea has occurred to many others too, and scores of people surround the buffet islands, forming queues. Were it not for the valuable works of art and grandiose view of the ocean through the alcove windows one would almost believe oneself in a self-service restaurant in a town ashore. Overnight the tired faces have assumed relaxed expressions reflecting the beginning of convalescence – the first night aboard has already worked small miracles. Armed with our plastic tray we join a queue. A wall disinfectant-wipe dispenser requests politely that we leave no traces on the cutlery. We make a mental note to rise thirty minutes earlier tomorrow to have a princely breakfast in the Britannia.

Once breakfast is over the day's programme is full of enticing ways to pass the time. Should we do a full circuit of the ship to find our way about and see what is on offer? We feel no real *urge* to do so. Experienced travellers have already identified this shipboard malady for us: 'There is jet lag. People know about it. It is unpleasant,' Hans-Christof Wächter wrote in his highly readable travel report *Transatlantische Passage*, explaining:

One needs at least a day to shed it. But there is nothing less researched than ship lag. That is pleasant, and therefore more pernicious, being more toxic. Its symptoms are lack of energy, inactivity, a wonderful feeling of sleepy-headedness, of weird strangeness. One simply desires to remain in this state perpetually without doing anything more except at certain time intervals to rise and eat exquisite food in fine surroundings. In the most extreme case the sufferer might watch some clay-pigeon shooting, gossip over a gin and tonic, wander the shops, buy some postcards (but without any clear determination to muster enough energy to write them). These brief outbursts of energy will lay the sufferer low again. With a happy sigh he will lower himself into a plush armchair, or a soft couch, open the voyage literature at the same page he has done for days and succumb to dreams, gazing at the rolling ocean and drifting clouds and cloudscapes.

Thus we find ourselves unintentionally in the Commodore Club, in one of those marvellous cream-coloured leather armchairs, drunk with the view through the man-sized windows of the sea and forecastle storeys below. A soft drink sparkles on the small table by the armchair and a deep, silent sigh escapes us at this sight. The impersonal changing theatre induces in us a certain tranquillity. Countless are the shades of colour in the movements of sea and cloud. Powerful deep blue, its small waves capped with white horses. A pale sky and cirrus. Sea glittering in the sunlight. A grey sky with fast-moving ribbons of cloud and blue-grey sea. A smooth, dark sea with a long swell under a yellowish sky after the last of the sunset. A confused sea, apparently wrestling with itself, oblivious of the great ship. And through these dream worlds *QM2* pursues her course calmly. She has a destination which she must reach even if we prefer to tarry. One realises that here lies the true reason why one must still cross the Atlantic by ship rather than aircraft, and why one prefers a transatlantic crossing to a Norwegian cruise – it gives one time. For those active in their careers, and who have chosen an exquisite break aboard *QM2*, the sweet luxury of loafing is certainly one of the main attractions of such a voyage.

Yet one should not think that *QM2* has nothing to offer but inactivity (more easily available at the seaside), for sooner or later the internal batteries will be recharged. One has conversed, got to know a few people and aroused the desire to undertake something with new acquaintances or 'friends whom one has just met'. A feeling of friendship and closeness which connects those aboard is almost universal.

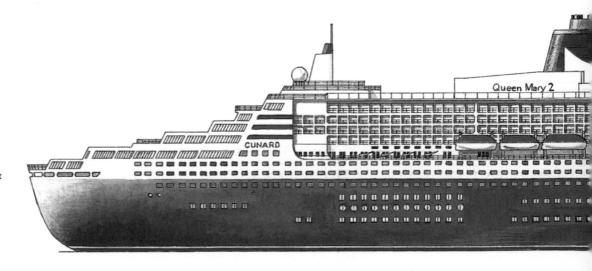

QM2 drawn by
**Dietmar Borchert
to 1:1000 scale**

Strangers suddenly exchange rare details of their lives and circumstances as if they had known each other for years. Friendships are quickly made aboard and dissolve at the destination just as quickly without anybody taking it amiss. Perhaps behind it all is simply the desire to share pleasant times with people in whose presence one feels comfortable.

Thus already during the first day at sea one tends to follow one's own agenda, which is pursued for the remainder of the voyage with a few minor changes as if it were the most natural thing in the world. We came aboard with the plan to have no plan, and in reality we have none, and simply pursue our personal need for the right mixture of rest, diversion and conversation and to satisfy our appetite for good food. One should therefore not be surprised that on clear, warm days the after-deck is well covered with deckchairs for snoozing or chat.

The Promenade Deck circuit is the domain of the joggers, who make their rounds untiringly from morning to evening. On smaller ships they form the contingent of most feared passengers, defending their right of passage if necessary by the use of elbows and other body parts. Aboard *QM2* the deck is broad enough to allow joggers and strollers to coexist peacefully. Walkers have

never resolved the centuries-old problem of the deck greeting. While promenading one will meet the same people circulating in the opposite direction. On the first encounter one will exchange polite greetings, on the second one may nod or exchange a word. But nearly all passengers express ignorance of how to behave the third time round. Should the parties ignore each other? Attempt to exchange glances? If the important thing is fresh sea air and a wonderful view then one's private balcony beckons, but there one is restricted, and one needs the variety to be found on deck.

At the stroke of midday the two foghorns roar as a prelude to the Commodore's announcement. He provides a nautical summary of the last twenty-four (or twenty-five) hours and gives the ship's position and the mileage covered. In days of yore the latter was of great importance, for the Pool – betting on the mileage – was the most popular 'book' aboard the old ocean liners, and even today one can place a bet on the daily run. The weather forecast is followed by special announcements – the sighting of dolphins, or a toast to Her Majesty on one of her birthdays, for example.

Ah, time for a dry sherry before lunch. We choose the Chart Room for its proximity to the

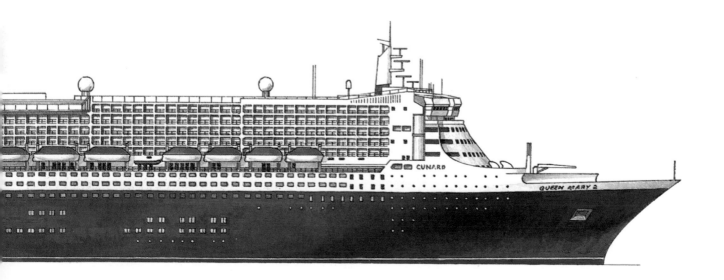

A 'flee market' regularly put up in the main corridor does not quite blend in with its luxurious surroundings but proves popular nonetheless

AUTHOR

Britannia Restaurant. After dining one either takes to a deckchair to enjoy the pleasant heaviness induced by culinary delicacies, or keeps moving and finds an afternoon activity. Wächter writes:

If one looks more closely at the Daily Programme, one will see that the overlapping crazy mixture of directed, undirected, supervised, led and accompanied activities are part of a system. There are five categories, which we can identify as: (1) intellectual meandering, (2) creative ideas, (3) social games, (4) sports and (5) cultural pursuits. Deep thought, boredom and dryness are the deadly sins. One can permit his mind to travel a little, but marathons are not encouraged.

The many maritime paintings and the (not totally convincing) Maritime Quest invite a maritime tour of discovery. The many works of art with which the *QM2* is adorned often demand that one stop to admire with a mind free of encumbrances. When would one have time to do that ashore? There is even a well-hidden Homer Simpson sketch in one of the works. Virtually around the clock one finds a rich choice of music for all tastes, be it violin or

The Britannia Restaurant

CUNARD

piano concerts in the Royal Court Theater, salsa in the Pavilion Pool, pop in the Golden Lion Pub, jazz in the Commodore Club or a harpist in the Chart Room.

One can be more active, of course: the performers of the Royal Academy of Dramatic Art not only present a show almost every evening but are ready to share their experience in courses where one can learn to speak from the stage or learn small parts. Guest lecturers voyage with the *QM2* to instruct interested passengers in the secrets of origami, watercolours and suchlike. Shipboard quizzes hosted by the staff offer diversion to those who prefer not to have to learn. Literature, music, films and TV – the categories are superficial and entertaining. To remind us we are aboard a British ship, lessons in bridge and the daily bingo sessions are high on the agenda. Sporting enthusiasts can enter the table tennis tournament at the Pool, practise on the golf simulator or play classic shuffleboard. And for 'a few' coins one can round this all off with a massage in the Canyon Ranch Spa Club.

The regular lectures in the Planetarium are not necessarily about the stars. With its video screens, Illuminations has an outstanding auditorium in which to hear guest speakers whose deliveries will be interesting and often entertaining. We are on vacation, though, and are happy not to be overwhelmed with too many facts. Not so hard to digest and richer are the meals aboard *QM2*, and whoever is keen to learn more of the culinary arts can take part in a wine or cheese appreciation course.

Aboard *QM2* it is difficult not to establish contact with fellow passengers. In order to guarantee that even the most introverted will find conversation partners if they so desire, the staff offer a number of events whose only aim is to bring people together. Traditionally there is a Singles Party for lone travellers, but former *Queen Mary* passengers and devotees of classical literature are also catered for. For most voyagers these separate threads come together in the late afternoon when the British institution of tea is celebrated in the Queens Room or King's Court restaurant.

We take our tea in style in the Queen's Room to the playing of a three-man orchestra. Lulled by soft music, we watch as white-gloved stewards move busily among the tables, serving tea. Others carry large silver trays filled with delicacies. Will they spoil one's appetite for dinner? If only they didn't look quite so tempting! Scones and clotted cream topped with strawberry jam may not be to everybody's taste, but those tiny salmon and cucumber sandwiches – how *can* one resist? And the *petits fours*, truffle sweets, do melt so sweetly in the mouth that it would simply be a sin to dismiss the steward before his silver tongs transferred just a few more to your plate.

Evening dance in the Queens Room

CUNARD

An odd phenomenon occurs after teatime: decks and rooms are deserted, all but a few guests vacate the bars and only an occasional passenger is to be found wandering abroad; most have vanished. Only in the restaurants is there life. The last items of cutlery are laid on the tables, the *maître* casts his eye over the glasses for cleanliness and sparkle, the last menu sheets for dinner are tucked into their holders. The ship prepares herself for evening. Since the Britannia Restaurant dines in two sittings, guests of the late sitting may see an early-evening show in the

theatre or a film in Illuminations. The first sitting is cabin-bound, dressing for the glitter and sparkle of the *QM2* evening programme.

On transatlantic voyages the Daily Programme states that the dress code is *formal*. This means that the jeans of the first evening are out, and the traveller is now faced with one of the most difficult questions of the voyage: what shall I wear? While male passengers have the relatively easy choice of dark suit or smoking jacket with suitable waistcoat, tie and so forth, the ladies have the potential for a drama should another female passenger have the same attire. So what shall it be, evening gown or cocktail dress? Which shoes? Will the silver necklace go with the dress? And the hair. Loose or piled up? Would a tiara be just too much?

Decisions made, in the early evening the passengers gradually make their appearance and at last we recognise that we are aboard a ship with status. Seated in an armchair in the Grand Lobby, it is a delightful spectacle to see elegantly clothed couples, many displaying the noblest evening wear their wardrobes have to offer. Society has not yet lost its sense of style – or at least not aboard the *QM2*. 'Ships that pass in the night are soon forgotten, but nights that pass in a ship are remembered forever,' wrote the American maritime historian John Maxtone-Graham, quoting an unknown source. And even today, nights aboard the *QM2* are unforgettable.

If dinner was once the highlight of the day, nowadays it is a rather quieter banquet. What levels of society do we have travelling with us? Who is the richest man aboard? Who is honoured by a seat at the Captain's table? These were once the matters of importance discussed by first-class passengers at dinner. On the *Normandie*, the Grande Salle à Manger was a majestic hall with mirrors, tall columns of light and an entrance platform almost as long as the hall itself – the ideal setting to 'see and be seen', at least in First Class. Second Class was formal, but Third Class had the mass appeal. King's

Court sends its greetings. In classless modern voyages these matters no longer carry the same weight. One is not so much under observation, although one likes to be seen.

We enter the Britannia Restaurant. Waiters station the chair correctly, spread a napkin on the lap and flourish the menu and wine list. What will it be this evening? The hors d'oeuvres have us salivating merely by looking through the menu. Smoked salmon in the oriental style with lemon dressing. Cold noodle salad with sesame. Crab on mango slices. Or should we have a consommé? Cuban bread salad on avocado? White wine? Between the courses there is an interval allowing the slowest eaters to finish their meals at leisure, to savour the flavour and enjoy a conversation at table.

The main course, the entrée, follows. Our taste-buds have been stirred. The tenderest Angus steak is swept in on a serving dish. Or breast of duck in Teriyaki sauce with new potatoes. Or perhaps sir would prefer pan-roasted medallions of lamb with glazed onion and artichoke hearts. On a transatlantic voyage, restoring one's inner equilibrium and great pleasure go hand in hand. After dessert (or should we be extravagant and have two?) has rounded off dinner gloriously, the second part of the evening recreation begins.

From James Cameron's cinema epic about a sunken luxury liner of long ago we know that at this point men of breeding left their female consorts to their own devices and retired to port wine and cigars in the Smoking Saloon, that

In the late evening, QM2 becomes the brightest star on the ocean

AUTHOR

**An extract from the annual
requirements of the *QM2*'s
restaurants:**

1.35 million tea-bags

55,000lb coffee

1.728 million eggs

38,000lb smoked salmon

**346,000 gallons of fruit
juice**

249,000lb potatoes

540,000 toothpicks

90 tonnes of pineapple

**... and an extract from the
technical specifications:**

**1,550 miles of electrical
cable**

80,000 light bulbs

**280,000 square yards of
fitted carpet**

**144,000 square yards of
insulation material**

3,000 telephones

8,800 loudspeakers

5,000 steps

5,000 smoke alarms

8,350 sprinklers

male bastion to which women were never admitted until long after the First World War. Nowadays the possibilities are greater and there is no reason for sexual discrimination unless at the passenger's own choice. Today Churchill's Cigar Lounge beckons the lover of high-quality tobacco, but that is something for later.

We leave the restaurant in excellent spirits with our companions at table. A rare glance at the clock – one of the few time checks of the day – tells us that the Royal Academy of Dramatic Art's performance begins in a few minutes in the Royal Court Theater. We lengthen our stride through the broad corridor leading from the Britannia Restaurant through the Grand Lobby to the Showlounge. Whatever the Daily Programme promised for today, the entertainment will be good, whether a review of well-loved musicals or Oscar Wilde's *The Importance of Being Earnest*. And the best is that after it finishes we shall still have a large part of the evening before us.

There is a good crowd in the Golden Lion Pub. A darts game is in progress. Your score is not so important as the company you find. We are lucky to get a table and enjoy a freshly drawn pint of beer. The karaoke party is in full swing. A comic disappoints but it is impressive to see the hidden talent exposed by the spotlights. Only superficial conversation is possible here; the noise swamps it.

In the Queens Room there is dancing. The Gentlemen Hosts – honourable single gentlemen of cosmopolitan character, no longer young, who are engaged by the company to balance the notorious surplus of females adept at classical dancing – have made their entrance. Their voyage and board are free and they have all the comforts and rights of paying passengers – except that in the evening

they are duty-bound to make themselves available as dance partners to the ladies in the Queens Room. In the neighbouring G32 Club special dance skills are not necessary: a DJ plays 'oldies' and disco sounds to dance to. After our happy couple of hours in the Golden Lion we feel like a quieter end to the evening. Passing the Empire Casino with its ceaseless rattle of slot machines, we take the lift to Deck 9. Here, at the forward end of the ship, a few decks below the bridge, is the tasteful Commodore Club. While it is a frequent criticism of cruise ships that music in the public rooms is so loud as to make normal conversation impossible, this can hardly be said of the Commodore Club. True, the loudspeakers here do pour out pop and jazz, but the volume is so low that conversation is not defeated.

Above the bar counter, thin neon tubes glow as in some American diner. Behind the bar is the imposing illuminated model of the *QM2* in a glass case. Seated in comfortable armchairs, we order a round of cocktails from the good-humoured waiters and engage in conversation with our new shipboard friends. So brief an acquaintance, so much to tell, and it seems we have been together for weeks. After the third round of drinks the steward discreetly requests last orders. We have failed to notice how time has flown. And after bar and ship model have been dimmed ...? We have long felt ready for bed but the night is still young. We stroll along the Promenade Deck, ignoring the fresh wind at this hour, which plays havoc with clothing and coiffure. The sky is deep black, the sea too. Only where the interior light from hundreds of portholes and windows falls on the water does one see the characteristic white greyness of the seas where the ship cleaves her path, and hear the whisper of the ocean through which *QM2* hammers out her distinct tempo. After this last ventilation of the lungs we finally bid our friends goodnight and retire to our cabin.

The kindly steward has already switched on the light, removed the daytime bedspread and

The high point at the end of the voyage: the sun rises behind the Manhattan skyline

AUTHOR

shaken the quilt. On the pillow are small tablets of chocolate in a white wrapping bearing the Cunard logo. Without spectacles this is easy to overlook. John Maxtone-Graham mentions this in his articles on the world of cruising by asking his public if they ever awoke one morning with a 'blood-smeared head' which smelt of chocolate. No doubt this evoked a grin or two. Impossible to miss, however, is a notice the size of a postcard, reminding us to put back the clock one hour before sleeping. Sleep is rarely so sound as aboard a westbound transatlantic liner, and the time difference grants us the occasional extra hour. The day aboard *Queen Mary 2* has twenty-five hours, and we enjoy every one of them. With these last thoughts we wrap ourselves in a soft blanket and let the ship rock us to sleep as if in a gigantic cradle.

Happily the voyage has still some way to go. Who knows what pleasant mental and tranquillising activities await us tomorrow? Yet just when it seems that the days stretch ahead, and one has gone to bed with the comforting thought that there is heaps more time, suddenly the last day at sea dawns. Although it begins as peaceably as those preceding it, by midday there seems to be an undercurrent of unrest. Can people smell the land, or know here it lies? Perhaps it is simply that now they recall the purpose of coming, which had been cast aside. One or two write postcards, or deliver completed mail to the Purser's Office. The bill for the credit card must be checked. Many make a final visit to the Mayfair Shops surrounding the Grand Lobby, having finally decided upon buying the trinket they noticed a few days earlier.

The packed sea trunk must be outside the cabin door by 2300. Packing is a job to be fitted in during the day, and then one has to resolve the question of tipping, one of the few problems

**At the end of the voyage:
QM2 at Red Hook Cruise
Terminal, Brooklyn**

AUTHOR

still to confront the Atlantic voyager. Cunard automatically charges $11 per person per day to the cabin account (although every guest has the right to reduce it if disgruntled). Nevertheless it is usual even today to reward with an extra tip all those who have taken special care of one.

The day is spent in strange hectic activity between the organisational (have we prepared all the entry formalities for the USA?) and the usual programme. Evening comes and we dress for dinner aboard for the last time. As the trunk had to be packed at an unreasonably early hour and we can only go ashore with hand luggage, the Daily Programme has announced that dress for the last evening will be casual. So suddenly they all reappear – the tourists whose wardrobe is really beyond the pale aboard *QM2*. Light slacks and a short-sleeved shirt without tie would have provided a breath of elegance, but unfortunately many think that 'casual' means 'anything'. We

shall not let anything spoil our evening, however. During a princely dinner we are introduced personally to all the busy hands in the stainless steel world of the ship's kitchens who prepared our culinary delights. Between entrée and dessert, wearing their tall white caps, they march in a long column through the Britannia Restaurant, line up at the step and reap their hard-won applause.

The table waiter presents every guest with an envelope containing the collection of menu cards as a souvenir of the voyage, and on that note the dinner ends. A slightly depressed air hangs over the evening's programme; one might almost say we are deflated, probably only by the knowledge that a few wonderful days – for many a once-in-a-lifetime experience – are now approaching their end, and that the time until our arrival in New York is measured in hours. Nobody wants to miss our entry into the port next morning, even though it will be at 0500.

Should we turn in early? Stay up all night? That would be going too far. Therefore we enjoy the offerings of the luxury liner for the last time and fall asleep late in a mixture of sorrow, pleasant relaxation and anticipation. All too early the alarm clock wakes us. We make the effort to arise, freshen up and go on deck. It fills rapidly. *QM2* is now moving through the water at a very modest speed: one did not feel the pulsing of the ship earlier, but now that it is gone one notices it.

There is still nothing to see. Deep darkness surrounds the ship and most early risers wander around aimlessly and dozily. What will be the best vantage point? We decide on Deck 13, whose broad open surface will give us the opportunity to move between port and starboard freely, while from this deck the passage below the Verrazano Narrows Bridge at the entrance to New York Bay will be seen at its most spectacular. The bridge is the first thing we make out through the darkness. A row of small points of light seems to block our way ahead. The closer we come, the more clearly we see the bridge, and finally we are so close that it seems it must be dangerously low. Ever closer the obstruction looms. Of course, everybody knows that even at high water and unladen, *QM2* still has ten feet of clearance for the funnel, but our eyes seem unconvinced. Ever nearer together come funnel and bridge and nothing can stop the colossus colliding with it – and then with an elegant curtsy *QM2* passes below the span. On the starboard bow the dawn streaks red, and as we watch a veil of colour tints the morning sky in the distance.

With increasing daylight we can make out the famous skyline of Manhattan, vague at first then extending outwards as we near. The sky above has colours besides the usual blue and glowing red: yellow, turquoise, olive, grey, pink and all manner of shimmering shades. We pass the illuminated Statue of Liberty to port and the ship turns just before Manhattan. All her illustrious predecessors went up the Hudson to the finger piers on the west side of Manhattan Island, but the liner leaves Manhattan to port, showing the city her long beam while bearing down on Red Hook in Brooklyn. Amid the industrial installations the berthing manoeuvre begins.

Most passengers have seen enough and leave the deck. We too go inside ('below deck', one would have said in the old days) to breakfast in the Britannia Restaurant and then fetch our hand luggage from the cabin. Somehow the experience is not quite 'real' any more. The ship comes to a stop, and in front of the windows one sees the wall of the terminal building. Already the crew has started the turnaround. The gangways are teeming with passengers and stewards while cleaners are already at work in the vacated cabins. We proceed to the almost ghostly casino to await disembarkation, and join our group. Passengers leave the ship by group to avoid overly long queues at Immigration.

When we are finally requested to leave the ship we see again that same sideways glance we observed at boarding. Suddenly we are standing with our luggage in front of the Red Hook Cruise Terminal. Looking back, we see how the building is dwarfed by the majestic liner. Limousines drive up, buses stand nearby. We load our bags into a yellow cab and after a final look back are driven off through a desolate industrial area. Within hours the *QM2* will sail for Southampton with a fresh batch of passengers. By then the staff will have thoroughly cleaned all cabins and public rooms, shipped supplies and fuel, removed all traces of our presence. The experience of the transatlantic passage, however, will remain with us for many years, and in dreams we imagine how it would be to sail with her again.

A few more statistics:
- Enough toilet paper is used aboard *QM2* yearly to circle the Earth five times.
- 1.5 million drinks are poured annually, not including 230,000 bottles of wine.
- The yearly consumption of beef on the *QM2* equals that of Southampton.
- If the full sacks of flour used aboard annually were stacked in a single column, it would stand five times higher than the Eiffel Tower.
- The ship has 34,500 square feet of kitchens.

CHAPTER

5

A magazine was published to
mark the visit of *QM2*
in Hamburg in 2005

CJP HAMBURG GMBH

A great procession escorts
QM2 out of the port of
Hamburg

RUDOLF GRIMME

HAFENCITY HAMBURG 01 AUGUST 2005
QUEEN MARY 2 DAY
Magazin

HSH NORDBANK *präsentiert*
QM 2 DAY
HAMBURG
Die Stadt am Wasser feiert
die Königin der Meere
Feiern Sie mit!
www.QM2DAY.de

THE
'QM2
IN
HAMBURG'
PHENOMENON

The city was baking hot as the ocean giant came in sight at 1100 hours that morning in July. She was the largest passenger ship ever to enter Hamburg, and the previous day the visit had been in doubt because the tide in the river Elbe was so low: it had been the hottest July on record and the prevailing easterlies brought little water. Mist had detained the liner at Copenhagen, and she was now a good two hours late. The band of the Hamburg Waterways Police had not assembled – too many of its members were on summer leave – and neither did the fire boats attend for the traditional greeting of firing plumes of water into the air. The Mayor of Hamburg, Helmuth Kern, had seen no compelling reason to squander money in this way, explaining that there was no precedent.

The liner was therefore escorted only by private yachts and boats as she made fast to the Überseebrücke (overseas landing stage). During the day the people of Hamburg turned out in their thousands to see the greatest passenger ship Hamburg had ever seen – reason enough for Captain William J Law to tell journalists that the ship had not had such a reception in any city before. When the vessel came back to the Elbe a year later, 20,000 sightseers were waiting. The ship was moored for thirty-one hours at the Überseebrücke and caused wails of disappointment from the city's business fraternity nevertheless: too few of the mainly British and American visitors had gone ashore, and those who did disembark for an excursion had not spent much.

Those who experienced the first two calls of *QM2* to Hamburg in July 2004 and August 2005 may frown and think rather of the mass hysteria surrounding a great event, yet neither of the first two visits of *QE2* to the Elbe in July

1972 and August 1973 had been anything like so spectacular. In the Germany of 1972 a new transatlantic liner was something of a relic with a doubtful future. Hapag-Lloyd had sold its flagship *Bremen*, and *Europa* had recently made her last Atlantic crossing and gone over exclusively to cruising. The Deutsche Atlantik Line had fitted out its new ship *Hamburg* with the technical necessities of a transatlantic liner, but was using her for pleasure cruises only. While the French *France* and the Italian *Michelangelo* and *Raffaello* held true to their purpose, these renowned ships were turning increasingly to pleasure cruising because the Atlantic was unprofitable.

What would Britain want with a ship like the *QE2*? Possibly many sightseers went to the harbour to see the liner once before her short

21 July 1972: *QE2* in Hamburg for the first time

STEFAN BEHN COLLECTION

When *QM2* left Hamburg on
the morning of 20 July 2004,
nobody yet suspected what
an important visit this had
been for the city

AUTHOR

career ended in the breaker's yard. While this
last thought may be a little 'over the top' the
cool reception the ship received in Hamburg
certainly was no incentive for a third visit, and
for the next seventeen years *QE2* avoided the
city, and even her four visits between 1990 and
1994 were dockyard lay-ups at Blohm + Voss.
Meanwhile the *QE2* had become an icon to
ship-lovers and those nostalgic for 'the good old
days'. On each of these latter occasions greater
interest was shown in her by the people and
media – and this was certainly the reason why
from 1996 onwards the old liner paid more calls
to the Hanseatic city. That *QM2* in her first year
of service would also visit Hamburg, whose
development as a commercial cruise-ship port
was in its infancy, was grist to the mill of the
press – for too long had the city ignored its
potential in this respect and been punished for it
financially.

Coinciding with the visit of the new
Cunarder, the new – provisional – Hamburg
Cruise Center was completed. The restructuring
of parts of Hamburg's old free-port warehouse
district into a harbour city had just begun and

the completion of a permanent cruise-ship
terminal was scheduled for 2009. The motive to
make Hamburg a booming passenger port was
such that in 2004 it required only two months
to make a departure hall on the Grasbrook area
out of fifty-one containers. It was opened to the
public a few weeks before the arrival of *QM2* by
A'rosa Blu of Aida Cruises (a subsidiary of
Carnival Corporation). Weeks before the *QM2*'s
arrival this event was being hailed as 'the greatest
event of the summer'. Estimates put the likely
number of sightseers at between 100,000 and
300,000. It was forecast that river traffic would
be so heavy that one 'would be able to cross the
Elbe without getting one's feet wet'. To people
coming from outside Hamburg, tourist agencies
offered special packages of an overnight hotel
stay and breakfast on a river steamer 'which
would pass close by the *QM2*'. Over 10,000
tickets were already sold for ninety launches and
fifteen large excursion ships.

The nearer the date came, the more detailed
was the reporting by Hamburg newspapers of
the strict security measures, indications of
remaining seating on launches, the best vantage

points, the estimated arrival times and news about the ship herself. *QM2* seemed to make Hamburg vibrate. The liner would arrive at Hamburg in the early morning of 19 July 2004. The previous evening hundreds of caravans were already positioned in parking places near the Elbe. In the morning the viewing points from Cuxhaven to the Hamburg fish market and landing bridges filled quickly with sightseers. It seemed that even at this early hour Hamburg was at the heart of a great event. Shortly after six, onlookers heard the deep roar of the ship's foghorns for the first time, and soon the contours of the *QM2* became visible through the morning mist.

Seldom had so large an assembly been so calmly and peaceably united to witness an event. An estimated 300 ships and boats escorted the *QM2* to her berth, kept at a respectable distance by the Waterways Police. Captain Paul Wright, commanding the liner, stated later in his report that he had never known such a welcome in his life and added jokingly: 'I blew the whistle continuously to waken the last of the sleeping passengers!' The steam pipes of *QM2* were never

The visit of QM2 brought tens of thousands to the Hamburg Cruise Center

THORBEN KOCKS

silent for long this morning. Every ship and boat with a siren greeted the ocean giant, and on every occasion *QM2* answered with three deep bass blasts.

On the Grasbrook, where the ship later moored, there was a carnival atmosphere all day. A never-ending stream of visitors walked the streets to the terminal, now well protected by police and wire fencing. Beyond its limits hot-dog booths, souvenir tents, beer stands, a stage with live music and mobile toilets had been set up. The post office quickly sold out of envelopes bearing a special *QM2* stamp. The number of telephone enquiries to the local Cunard agency asking if visits aboard were possible could not even be estimated. According to media reports, 400,000 sightseers came from all over Germany just to see the ship between the day of her arrival and the following morning. A great fireworks display brought it all to a close. At first light next morning *QM2* cast off from the Hamburg Cruise Center, turned precisely in her manoeuvring circle off the Grasbrook and headed down the Elbe for the next stage of her voyage, accompanied once more by countless

QM2 and Hamburg: always an impressive combination

AUTHOR

boats and yachts and waved off by thousands ashore. The Cunard Line's German client magazine proclaimed that 'the affair between the city and the Cunard Queen had become a great love story'.

The city fathers, the Cunard agency in Hamburg and even Captain Wright believed that such a visit had to be repeated, yet apart from the planned docking at Blohm + Voss in November the following year, the published schedules included no future visit by *QM2* to the Elbe (although *Queen Elizabeth 2* was due to make two calls there in 2005). Less than six months later it was announced that the itinerary had been changed. On the Norwegian cruise the following summer, *QM2* was due to call at Stavanger when returning from Geirangerfjord to Southampton, but the ship's speed made it possible to drop Stavanger and visit Hamburg instead on 1 August 2005. Those who thought nothing could match the enthusiasm of 2004 were mistaken. To quote a headline, Hamburg went 'mad for Mary'. Even the city council now realised the enormous potential connected to the ship's visits. On the first occasion the visit had been celebrated mainly on the Grasbrook. Now

it seemed that the phenomenon would spread over the whole city. CJP Hamburg GmbH, commissioned to organise the event, called it '*QM2* Day'. Financed by sponsors, everybody now wanted a slice of the cake. A magazine and merchandising were distributed especially for the visit. The call of *QM2* in 2005 generated 50 million euros a boost for the economy and valuable publicity for the city of Hamburg.

The media did its best to whip up the euphoria. For days the newspapers led with the *QM2* story, replacing the cycling race 'HEW Cyclassics', which had dominated the front pages at this time in previous years. It was the month of the summer holidays in Germany, and those who had missed the excitement the first time around wanted to be there this time. Excursions to and from the Elbe were virtually sold out days in advance. Thousands thronged the river banks as at 0500, when it was still dark, *QM2* passed the landing stage. The local TV station Hamburg 1 broadcast twenty-four hours on the liner's arrival, and the Grasbrook hosted a livelier programme than in 2004.

Captain Bernard Warner on the bridge of *QM2* was no less impressed than his colleague Wright had been the year before. If one mentions Hamburg on board the ship today, the eyes of those crew members who witnessed the event light up. Ever since, the German press has called Hamburg 'the secret home port of the ship'. A particular highlight was the turning manoeuvre in which *QM2* prepared for the voyage downstream. With an eye to the watching public, instead of making the turn immediately prior to sailing, towards midday the liner cast off from the Hamburg Cruise Center on the Grasbrook, turned through 180 degrees without tug help and moored again.

Although '*QM2* Day' as good as paralysed all traffic around the harbour all day, the mood of friendliness which dominated the carnival was impressive. It was estimated that the Cunarder lured a half million visitors to see her on 1

Shortly before midnight on
1 August 2005, *QM2* sailed
from Hamburg – the high
point of an exciting day

THORBEN KOCKS

August 2005. Towards midnight, when she cast off for the last leg of her journey to Southampton, all vantage points were so crowded that the police sealed off the floating pontoons of the landing bridges and closed entry into the underground railway stations to prevent crushes. A few days before, the newspaper *Hamburger Abendblatt* had sold quantities of 'cable lights' (those small plastic tubes which light up when the tube is bent and two chemicals inside mix), and the banks of the Elbe were lit by countless green dots of light. As the *QM2* moved slowly past the huge crowds, the skies were lit by 'Hamburg's longest fireworks display' from various sites along seven miles of river.

That *QM2* was due to dock at Blohm + Voss in November was already known (see Chapter 3), and this was a further incentive for bookings. A later docking in May 2006 coincided with the anniversary of the harbour, in which the liner was the 'star guest'. By then 'QM2 Day' had become an institution: for 2006 there were two

scheduled visits to Hamburg on the itinerary. To keep the events under control, city managers ashore were now having to plan carefully.

Rather more modest was the visit of 16 July 2006, a Sunday with sun and clear skies, when the Grasbrook teemed with 200,000 spectators awaiting the liner's arrival. The expectations for the visit of 25 August were exaggerated, however, when days before the newspapers published under a banner headline 'Queen meets Dreamship' the news that the great Cunarder would visit Hamburg at the same time as the flagship *Deutschland* of the Peter Deilmann shipping company of Neustadt in Holstein. (The headline referred to the fact that the *Deutschland* played the main role in the German TV equivalent to *Love Boat*, *Traumschiff*.) Although the atmosphere of a great event prevailed and about 60,000 attended, numbers were clearly down. Even this turnout was impressive, however, when one considers that this was the sixth visit of the liner to

Impressive comparisons of size as *QM2* lies alongside the Phoenix Reisen-operated *Alexander von Humboldt* at the Hamburg Cruise Center, 16 July 2006

Hamburg within two years.

During the day Captain Warner visited his colleague Kapitän Hubert Flohr aboard *Deutschland*. On the Grasbrook the usual souvenir and fast-food stands had been set up, and in the afternoon seven choirs aboard a lighter in the harbour performed traditional sea shanties from Gemany's age of sail. The north German radio station NDR 90.3 and the *Hamburger Abendblatt* had asked people to choose their five favourites from a list. At the end of the renditions, all 250 singers of the choirs sang the five songs selected to take leave of the two passenger ships.

Towards 1800 *Deutschland* sailed. At 575 feet she is only half as long as the *QM2*, and at only 22,496 gross tons a dwarf compared with the Cunard giant. Passing the landing stage she pleased onlookers by releasing hundreds of black, red and gold balloons from her forward hatch. *QM2* followed half an hour later and delighted the crowds with the deep groan of her

two foghorns. Cunard now recognised that in no other port in the world did the *QM2* win such publicity for the company by her mere presence as in Hamburg, and it came as no surprise that two visits there were included in the ship's 2007 itinerary – worked into the transatlantic passages to New York via Southampton.

Anyone who wanted to see the *QM2* in motion on the water had to be a night owl or a very early riser. On 26 July 2007, commanded by Captain Christopher Rynd, *QM2* visited Hamburg from 0400 until shortly before midnight. The celebrations of the previous year were repeated, although '*QM2* Day' in July was a fairly restrained affair so as not to overshadow the visit of 23 August, when more was to be offered the public. The 2008 dates of 30 July and 27 August are already marked in the diaries of those for whom the '*Queen Mary* in Hamburg' phenomenon had become a fixed ritual.

Cunard used the publicity and the love of the

Hamburg population for the ship to present the new *Queen Victoria*: as part of her maiden voyage to the Christmas markets of northern Europe, the newest addition to the Cunard fleet was scheduled to visit Hamburg on 18 December 2007.

As a sort of appetiser to this event the *QE2* was to have paid a visit to Hamburg ten days earlier. However, due to stormy weather the river pilot could not board the vessel, so that the call to Hamburg was omitted and the vessel set course to Oslo. The city was thus deprived of its final chance to say farewell to the venerable old liner which it had greeted so timidly thirty-five years previously, but had learned to love as time had passed.

In Hamburg whenever *QM2* visits, ship-fever

The Queen meets the 'Traumschiff' the German TV equivalent of the 'Love Boat': on 25 August 2005, *QM2* shared a berth with the *Deutschland*

AUTHOR

breaks out, the city stands on its head and for the uninvolved spectator it is all too easy to forget that the arrival of a ship of this or any other calibre requires regulations. Behind the stage, the *QM2* is a ship like any other. Her true purpose is not to make the people of Hamburg happy, but to satisfy the paying passengers. To that extent everything must go like clockwork. As the planned voyages of the *QM2* are worked out well in advance by Cunard, the planning and preparation of the Hamburg visit can begin early. About a year before the planned arrival the berth for the liner will be reserved at the

Hamburg Cruise Center. For this purpose Cunard informs its shipping agent of the planned date and time of arrival, and the ports to be visited immediately before and after Hamburg. The shipping agent is as a rule a company located in a port whose employees know the local circumstances. Bearing in mind the enormous number of ports visited by cruise ships nowadays, it would be a mammoth task for every shipping company to know and keep in touch with all the authorities and suppliers of services at every port in the world.

The shipping agent – for Cunard the firm of Sartori & Berger – represents Cunard in all logistical and official matters, ensures smooth communication between everybody involved and looks after ship and crew during the visit to the port. It also arranges security at the terminal and police co-ordination with other events, and advises the company and ship's staff on all important questions. After receipt of the first information, Sartori & Berger contact the operators of the cruise terminal in Hamburg. Once they have checked on availability, the berth is reserved for the period required. In the autumn of each year a reservations plan for the Cruise Center is drawn up and a copy sent to the Hamburg Port Authority.

Meanwhile Sartori & Berger send Cunard the first estimate for the port charges based on ship size etc, but also on what the terminal will be required to supply (e.g. gangways, fork-lift trucks, personnel), and whether Hamburg is to be an intermediate stop or there will be a changeover of passengers. The agent receives a port questionnaire so that logistical and touristic details can be worked out: information about road connections, public transport, church services, places to eat or where the nearest golf course is. The shipping agent is the front-line office for practical matters. With a new ship it has to be ascertained whether the Elbe will have sufficient water at all states of the tide to float her. With her draught of over thirty feet, the

QM2 cannot pass over the 'Alter Elbtunnel' (the old tunnel beneath the river Elbe near the landing stage) at low tide. In order not to run aground or damage the tunnel it is absolutely essential to prepare a window for the passage dependent on the tide. The positioning of the gangways, the height of shell doors in the hull, and the issue of whether the company will require porterage for passengers or needs the ship to be reprovisioned: these all play a role in the preparations.

The 'hot phase' for the arrival at Hamburg begins about three weeks beforehand. As in the Hamburg harbour there are certain restrictions in force – the navigable channel in the Elbe has a maximum breadth of 295 feet in which two ships can pass – a ship over 1,080 feet in length and 147 feet in the beam is rated an 'extraordinarily large vessel'.

At least with regard to her length the *QM2* falls into this category, and although in these modern times of container-ship giants the number of 'extraordinarily large' ships visiting Hamburg has more than doubled in recent years, it is rare for such a ship to navigate the Elbe beyond the container terminals and into the city centre.

About three weeks before the arrival, Sartori & Berger give notice to the Hamburg Port Authority and submit the 'Official Request for Approval of the Waterways Police to enter Hamburg Harbour'. The document provides information regarding the size of the ship and the expected draughts at the expected times at various fixed points along the Elbe. The Hamburg Port Authority verifies this information with the details of previous visits by the ship, checks again that draught and tide conditions are in harmony and then issues an 'Exception Approval' for the 'extraordinarily large' Cunarder. The time window allowed the *QM2* for the passage over the Alter Elbtunnel is three hours either side of high water.

Since the conditions in Hamburg harbour are influenced by the conditions of flow in the Elbe, the Port Authority has to check whether the depth of water in the area to be navigated and in the turning circle where the *QM2* will manoeuvre through 180 degrees is sufficient. Any newly reported underwater obstruction will have to be removed. One to two weeks before the arrival, Sartori & Berger communicate with the ship to commence planning for the arrival in Hamburg. This will involve a mutual exchange of information including nautical data and details of the needs of ship and crew. For example, there is an obligatory minimum charge for discharging a certain amount of human waste and oil sludge. The ship is charged extra for any quantity of waste discharged beyond that. During its stay the ship may be refuelled, which has to be arranged, and its needs for fresh water, provisions and special goods can be met by the agent.

Three working days before the arrival at Hamburg, Sartori & Berger must forward the crew and passenger list to the Hamburg Waterways Police, under whose jurisdiction the customs handling of the ship falls. Crew members will be issued with short-term shore leave passes and preparations made for the disembarkation of passengers if required. As a consequence of the events of 11 September 2001 the International Maritime Organization (IMO) in London drew up the International Ship and Port Facility Security Code (ISPS) containing the minimum regulations for the security of ships in harbour The days when a few friendly words were enough to get one aboard ship in harbour for a look around are now gone. It is the port agent's responsibility to forward all the required documents – such as those related to in-port security or waste disposal – to the respective parties.

Twelve hours before arrival the terminal must declare 'clear ground', which means that the berth is free and that no other vessel or obstruction is in the area which could impede mooring or turning. A few hours later the ship

QM2 has sailed from Hamburg, but a return call is scheduled already

AUTHOR

passport was enough, and this was done during the run upriver. Under the new rules passenger and passport must be seen together if the passenger is proposing to go ashore. Off the remote city district of Blankenese the Elbe pilots hand the ship over to the harbour pilots, one of whom will have been a sea captain with high-seas experience and with knowledge of Hamburg harbour and the ships and obstructions within. A ship over 1,000 feet long can only be handled by pilots with at least ten years' such experience. Shortly before the arrival of QM2 at the pilot station the pilots will have consulted on how the ship will manoeuvre in. The Elbe is subject to currents at the berth and these play a role in the intended turning circle.

Equally significant but less amenable to calculation are the conditions of wind and visibility. For the QM2 wind strength must not exceed Force 7 with visibility of at least one kilometre. Especially when a captain is running into a port for the first time, perhaps even with a ship he has just taken over, he puts his trust in the harbour pilots much as the blind man does in his dog. Basically the Captain transfers his responsibility to the pilot. The psychological aspect of the pilot's job is as equally demanding as the technical one. The pilot assumes responsibility for the ship entrusted to him but also for the harbour.

Before the Elbe pilots leave the ship they provide their colleagues with the up-to-date radar picture and report the situation. The harbour pilots then discuss the procedure and situation in the harbour with the ship's Master. A magnet for the public such as the QM2 needs additional security while entering harbour. This is provided by the Waterways Police, who set up an exclusion zone around the ship with their police boats. It is important to keep the channel ahead of the ship free of inexperienced boat-handlers, yachtsmen and over-bold lightermen. To date all waterborne spectators have exercised good discipline.

will begin her run-in to Hamburg. Near light-buoy Elbe 1, about twenty sea miles off the estuary, two Outer Elbe pilots board the vessel. At this stage the harbour pilot station is informed of the impending arrival. The Outer Elbe pilots will normally hand over to the two Inner Elbe pilots off Brunsbüttel, at the mouth of the river, but because of the size of the QM2 the Outer Elbe pilots remain aboard with their colleagues until the ship reaches the boundaries of the port of Hamburg. Since Britain – the nation of registry of the QM2 – is not a signatory to the Schengen Agreement, the ship's passengers have to be processed by Immigration. For this purpose a tug is specially arranged, for that takes to the vessel two Hamburg Waterways Police officers, whose responsibility it is to prepare and process immigration procedures for passengers and crew as far as possible. These officials of the Waterways Police, who come aboard together with the Inner Elbe pilot, are accompanied by employees of Sartori & Berger, who will assist them with the procedures and – if need be – help overcome language barriers.

In former times mere sight of a passenger's

The collaboration of everyone involved has worked like clockwork. Passengers and crew look forward to sailing

AUTHOR

For *QM2* the most difficult part of her voyage to her berth begins near Blohm + Voss Docks 10 and 11 opposite the floating pontoons of the landing stage, where the channel is relatively narrow for a ship of this size, and moreover the Elbe has a bend here. In order remain manoeuvrable the liner must maintain momentum. Mooring at the Hamburg Cruise Center succeeds through co-operation between the Captain and pilots. Because the *QM2* has a small turning circle she requires tugs only in difficult weather conditions. For the pilots the job ends when the last mooring warp is in place. Two customs officers are the first to go aboard *QM2* once the gangway is secured. They receive the papers detailing the ship's cargo and the personal belongings of the crew. Customs may confirm these declarations by inspection if they so require. As soon as the Waterways Police have signalled readiness, passengers and authorised crew may disembark and the unloading of luggage begins.

At the ship's free side the waste chutes (usually for quantities of between 2,800 and 4,200 cubic feet) are attached, or a fuel barge may come alongside. At the quay the ship takes on freight and fresh water under the constant watch of customs officers, who upon completion sign off with approval for the voyage to continue. When the long day ends and *QM2* is ready to leave, the ship has to be cleared first by the Waterways Police. Organised by Sartori & Berger, workers stand by to release the mooring cables, the pilots come aboard and, if the weather requires it, tugs are prepared to take the hawsers. As with the approach into harbour, pilots and Waterways Police keep the channel clear for the voyage downstream. For the port agent the task is not yet completed. The cost of the ship's visit will be taken care of by the agent, and invoices controlled and eventually debited to the shipping company. Employees also attend to lost luggage and the disembarked mail.

If upon the arrival of *QM2* one asks people whether her visit is routine or something special, one gains the impression that whatever the personal feeling, ultimately she is just a ship. The preparations for despatch proceed surely and conscientiously – for routine, as all agree, is the enemy of alertness, and the process must not become routine.

C   H   A   P   T   E   R

6

QUEEN VICTORIA

'The period between the concept of a new Cunard Queen and the ship entering service has always been a source of trouble to the company in the past. *Queen Victoria* was no exception. Six years passed from the initial announcement to the maiden voyage. In the foregoing chapters we have seen how Cunard was taken over by the Carnival Corporation and the great mixed fleet gradually sold off in the restructuring process. Cunard was to be marketed henceforth as the original British luxury ship company. The renaming of *Vistafjord* as *Caronia* and placing her in Britain – still the world's second largest market for cruises – was an important step, although it was obvious this could only be an interim solution. *Caronia* had been built thirty years before and though well loved did not possess the same aura as *QE2*. If the Cunard fleet was not to be reduced further, a suitable replacement had to be found. To limit speculation, on 14 December 2001 Carnival

Corporation signed a Letter of Intent with the Italian yard Fincantieri to build a new ship for Cunard. The first release revealed that the new, unnamed Cunarder would be a cruise ship of about 85,000 gross tons and the second largest Cunarder ever built after the *QM2*. She would have two Azipods and diesel-electric drive, a continuous promenade deck around the ship, a lounge with a view over the forecastle, a pool

FINCANTIERI
ruise Ships

Holland America Line

Vista Class

Holland America Line's *Zuiderdam* is the prototype of the Vista Class

FINCANTIERI

with a 'Magradome' and glass lifts through ten decks on both sides of the ship, the usual accoutrements of the modern cruise ship. She would also have versions of the known and revered public rooms of *QE2*. 'This new vessel will exemplify the pinnacle of Italian shipbuilding today,' Francesco Guarguaglini, one of the Fincantieri directors, commented on the signing of the Letter of Intent. 'We are confident Fincantieri's craftsmen will delivery a truly splendid new Cunarder.'

Ship-lovers regretted that Cunard would only be adding a cruise ship to its fleet and not replacing *Caronia*, which was still suitable for the North Atlantic service. Carnival Corporation and the shipyard had developed a ship type suitable for all subsidiary lines and known as the Vista Class. The first two ships of this class

entered service in 2002 (*Zuiderdam*) and 2003 (*Oosterdam*) for the Holland America Line, while Carnival had an option on four others of the type for which the yard had capacity and resources. Yard No 6078 was earmarked for Holland America Line with a delivery date in January 2005, and Cunard was advised of the time window. The first computer graphics showed that the new Cunarder was similar to the Vista Class but the double funnel would be trunked into a modified version of the *QE2*'s single funnel, apparently now a Cunard trademark, and would be classic red above a black hull.

Speculation had begun about the name. With *QM2* and *Caronia* Cunard had reverted to historic names, and so *Mauretania* headed the betting. The first *Mauretania* had been the 'grandmother' of the Queens, so to speak, and the second ship of the name the 'smaller sister', and it was a well-known and historic name. All the greater was the surprise when on 31 March 2003 Cunard announced the name of the new Cunarder – *Queen Victoria*. The strategy was only seen here in hindsight in the light of the sale of the *Caronia*. Pamela Conover explained:

Cunard Line was founded just after *Queen Victoria* came to the throne, and her reign saw the company develop hugely in every sense. Throughout her reign Cunard built more and even better ships, we embraced radical new technology and we carried more passengers in greater comfort. Today, with more capacity than we have had for forty years, Cunard is entering a new phase of expansion commensurate with that experienced under *Queen Victoria*, so it seems entirely appropriate for the new ship to bear the name. It is also fitting that the second largest Cunarder ever should also bear a Queen name!

In the wake of Cunard's new direction in the home market, it was also stated that the *Queen Victoria* would sail under the British flag with

Southampton as her port of registry. The menus and entertainments would be tailored to British tastes. The pound sterling would be the shipboard currency, replacing the US dollar, which had been aboard Cunard ships for decades. This idea was eventually abandoned. The press announcement concluded by saying that the keel of the new ship would be laid in July 2003. One may assume that the board had

4 July – Cunard's anniversary date – in mind, but after the announcement of her name Yard No 6078 became something of a recluse. Because of all the current publicity about the *QM2* this was noticed by only a few, the others probably thinking that the Cunard management did not want the new order to steal the limelight of the *QM2*.

Queen Victoria was built in the Marghera yard

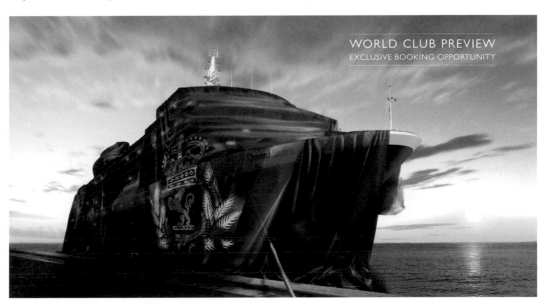

WORLD CLUB PREVIEW
EXCLUSIVE BOOKING OPPORTUNITY

Cunard marketed the newest addition to the fleet using this image

CUNARD, AUTHOR'S COLLECTION

An unpublished leaflet intended to introduce *Queen Victoria* Yard No 6078 to the public.

CUNARD, STEFAN BEHN COLLECTION

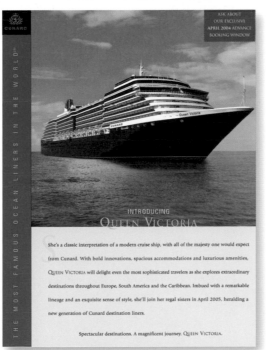

at Venice, which had been founded in 1923 by the industrialist Ernesto Breda. After nearly everything was destroyed in the Second World War, the yard was rebuilt much larger. After several changes of owner, in 1979 Marghera yard came under the control of the Fincantieri group, whose roots in shipbuilding extended back to the nineteenth century. The Fincantieri group claims to have built about 7,000 ships in its long history. It is today the greatest shipbuilder in Europe and fourth largest in the world. Its eight yards at various locations each specialise in particular technical fields but can combine their labour forces for major tasks. Cruise ships are built almost exclusively at Monfalcone, Marghera and Sestri Ponente near Venice. The last-named yard delivered the two most famous Italian ocean liners *Rex* and *Andrea Doria*. The other yards specialise in merchant ships of all kinds, very large yachts, warships, floating platforms and ship repairs. Marghera yard covers more than four million square feet. The building dock is 1,100 feet long and 177 feet wide and can take ships up to 250,000 gross tons. Since the beginning of the 1990s, when the increase in cruise-ship size seemed to have no limit, the yard contributed considerably to the enlargement of the world fleet, and besides the Vista Class it produced ships such as *Costa Classica, Costa*

The youngest Cunarder was built of blocks, using the modular construction method

FINCANTIERI

Romantica, Carnival Conquest, the luxury ferries *Pride of Hull* and *Pride of Rotterdam*, and the Disney sister ships *Disney Magic* and *Disney Wonder*. Cunard awarded the contract for furbishing the inner rooms to London's 'designteam'. After a foretaste on the *QM2* they would now show what they could do – an important contract for such a young firm.

If connoisseurs of Cunard expected that soon after the commissioning of *QM2* the Cunard publicity machine would start to run, and

bookings would be accepted for the first voyages of the *Queen Victoria*, they were mistaken. At the beginning of 2004 'flyers' were printed with the initial information about the new ship, in which mention was made that it might be possible to book voyages from April. These were described of as fifteen-day Mediterranean voyages in the summer of 2005 and fifteen-day voyages through the Panama Canal and to Hawaii, but nothing further was heard of them. Instead, on 5 April 2004, Cunard announced

that it had ordered a new ship from Fincantieri to be called *Queen Victoria*, and Yard No 6078 had been transferred to P&O Cruises.

As its reason for this step Cunard stated that the great success of *QM2*, particularly the demand for suites and junior suites, had shown that a more luxurious ship was needed. 'The design of the new *Queen Victoria* will be more consistent with the grand ocean liner style of *Queen Mary 2* and *Queen Elizabeth 2*,' Pamela Conover stated. 'We want to be sure that our

The bridge goes aboard

FINCANTIERI

The bow section – as yet lacking the name – of ship No 6127

FINCANTIERI

The squarish stern of *Queen Victoria*

FINCANTIERI

Queen Victoria at the fitting-
out quay, Fincantieri
shipyard, March 2007

JÜRGEN SAUPE

Floating of hull No 6127 on
15 January 2007

FINCANTIERI

new ship has all the luxurious Cunard attributes our clients expect.'

This indicated that Carnival Corporation was determined not to repeat the mistakes of the past and split the luxury into two classes. A further reason behind the decision to transfer hull No 6078 to P&O was that at the time of placing the order nobody had anticipated that the former competitor of April 2003 would join the Carnival Corporation. Cunard and P&O, two

British institutions with a long history, now stood side by side in the portfolio of the American conglomerate. In consequence there had to be a distinct and clear division in styles on board, and also of target clientele. Thus it seemed sensible for Cunard to pursue the beaten path of especially luxurious ships with a cosmopolitan ambience while P&O remained an uncertain entity for Carnival. Here the public would be lured henceforth with modern ships

The still-incomplete interior of the ship, January 2007

JÜRGEN SAUPE

Where would a Cunarder be without the characteristic funnel?

JÜRGEN SAUPE

having a mixture of styles.

After their takeover of hull No 6078, P&O announced that the ship would sail her maiden voyage in April 2005 under the name *Arcadia*. According to 'designteam' it should be possible to obtain a good idea from *Arcadia* of how this first *Queen Victoria* would have looked, because there were few modifications to the original designs. The children's nursery and teenagers' club were turned into a Fitness Room because

the *Arcadia* is exclusively for passengers over eighteen. The second *Queen Victoria* received Yard No 6127. Cunard used the opportunity to make some modifications to the Vista Class and make the ship a better sea-keeper. The hull was lengthened by a few yards and strengthened at the bow. The *Queen Victoria* is not suitable for all-weather transatlantic service, but these changes and a twenty-six-foot draught are acceptable for good conditions. The square stern of the Vista Class was retained. In order to differentiate the ship a little from her stepsisters the bridge front was redesigned.

There was now a long lull. The *Queen Victoria* was never mentioned on the Cunard Internet site. Even within the company there were questions as to where management was headed with the project. Not until almost a year later did the new ship appear on the back page of the main British Cunard catalogue, announced for the summer of 2007. On 16 February 2006 the marketing programme began in earnest. A press communiqué gave details for the first time of the fitting-out of the public rooms of the new ship, now measuring 90,000 gross tons. The first computer graphics helped to provide an idea of how she would look. Carol Marlow, the new President and Managing Director of Cunard, was quoted as saying:

> **I'm delighted to be able to announce this magnificent addition to our fleet – Sir Samuel Cunard himself would have been rightly proud.**

Queen Victoria will be a classically styled Cunard Queen, offering the very best of our heritage, along with the luxury and modern day comforts our guests have come to expect. [….] Being the second largest Cunarder ever, Queen Victoria is perhaps not about size superlatives, but rather style superlatives.

The first two voyages were also announced. Much to the surprise of the experts, the maiden voyage was not to warmer climes or across the Atlantic but to the Christmas markets of northern Europe, and scheduled to begin on 11 December 2007, followed by a sixteen-day cruise to the Canaries before the *Queen Victoria* made her first Atlantic crossing to New York in tandem with *QE2* on 8 January 2008 – causing travellers who knew what the Atlantic could be like at that time of the year to wonder how the boxy design of the *Queen Victoria* would handle the possibly adverse weather conditions. Shortly afterwards came the confirmation that she would be named at Southampton on 10 December

UNEQUAL SISTERS

Essentially, P&O's *Arcadia* and Cunard's *Queen Victoria* are Vista Class, but in fact that the *Queen Victoria* is unique in the class is shown by the following comparison:

	Arcadia	Queen Victoria
Yard Number	6078	6127
Date commissioned	12.04.2005	10.12.2007
Tonnage	83,000 BRZ	90,000 BRZ
Length	285.3m/936ft	294m/964.5ft
Beam	32.3m/106ft	32.3m/106ft
Draught	8m/26.2ft	8m/26.2ft
Speed	22 knots	23.7 knots
Building cost	£200 million	£300 million
Number of passengers	1,952	2,014
Number of cabins		
Interior	218	143
Exterior	73	146
With balcony	685	718

Hull 6078

Ship No 6078 was intended to enter service as *Queen Victoria*, but was commissioned by P&O as *Arcadia*

FINCANTIERI

2007, although no royal celebrity was mentioned in this connection.

On 19 May 2006 the preparatory stage had advanced sufficiently for the keel of Yard No 6127 to be laid. Carol Marlow and Commodore Warwick were invited as guests of honour to witness a small ceremony in which the first section, consisting of six 'blocks' weighing 325 tons altogether, was lifted into the building dock. Over the next few months further sections were added to this first piece and gradually *Queen Victoria* grew in length and height.

The next stage of construction was reached on 15 January 2007, when Yard No 6127 was ready to 'marry the sea' – to be floated in the building dock and removed under tow to the fitting-out quay to free the dock for a new ship. While the new Cunard construction had proceeded mostly unnoticed by the public up to this point, the event was marked by a celebration. In Italian shipbuilding it is a tradition to nominate a 'godmother' for the launching, of which the modern 'floating' is the equivalent. This honour

was given to the long-serving Cunard Line hostess Maureen Ryan. She joined Cunard in 1963 at the age of seventeen and is the only person known to have served guests aboard all former Queens. Today she continues with this work, and despite her invariable friendliness she has seen the seven seas and is not fooled easily. As *madrina* to the *Queen Victoria* she was now witness to the age-old tradition of laying two coins below the foot of the mast – a simple Italian euro coin symbolised the land in which this newest Cunarder was being built, and for Great Britain a gold Queen Victoria sovereign was added. At the conclusion of the ceremony a priest blessed the ship, Maureen Ryan smashed a bottle of Italian Prosecco against the hull, the dock was flooded, and the ship obeyed Archimedes' principle and rose gently from the support beams on which she had been constructed to be towed at once to the nearby fitting-out quay. For almost eleven months the yard workers and their subcontractors would now be engaged with the fitting-out of cabins,

During the building of Hull No. 6127 the vessel was registered to Nassau, Bahamas. This was later changed to the rightful homeport of Southampton, as is evident on the maiden voyage image on the right

RIGHT: JÜRGEN SAUPE
BELOW: KAI ORTEL

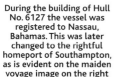

public rooms and crew areas, completing the technical installations, kitchens and decks to ensure that *Queen Victoria* would be ready at the beginning of December for delivery to Cunard.

The ship made her first sea trials on 24 August 2007. With almost 600 workers and experts aboard, all systems were subjected to capacity and endurance testing and extensive sea-keeping trials. In a press communiqué Cunard stated its satisfaction: 'The first trial voyage was a total success. As expected the new *Queen Victoria* is a fast, comfortable cruise ship with excellent qualities.' Even the internal furbishment was taking shape three months before the maiden voyage. The public rooms were already easily recognisable, and many corridors had been decorated and lighting installed. Work on the last details was begun in September. Both the Pavilion and Lido Pools,

24 August 2007: leaving for sea trials

RODOLFO CHISAM, HTTP://WWW.CROCIERISTI.IT

The *Queen Victoria* arrives at Southampton

CUNARD LINE

Cunard Line president Carol
Marlow, the Prince of Wales,
the Duchess of Cornwall and
Captain Paul Wright at the
apogee of events.

CUNARD LINE

Cunard Line president Carol
Marlow, the Prince of Wales,
the Duchess of Cornwall and
Captain Paul Wright at the
apogee of events.

CUNARD LINE

Humorous insight into the
history of the Cunard Line
was given by Shakespearian
actor Sir Derek Jacobi at the
naming ceremony.

CUNARD LINE

Before the christening the
vessel was blessed by the
Archbishop of Canterbury

CUNARD LINE

It is the maiden voyage – so
not everything is perfect
yet!

MARTIN GRANT

and the Whirlpools, had been extensively tested.

The guessing game as to who would name the ship officially was ended on 10 September 2007 when Cunard announced that HRH the Duchess of Cornwall had accepted its invitation.

On 24 November 2007 the *Queen Victoria* officially began her career with Cunard when she was handed over to the line at the Fincantieri Marghera yard. The event was marked by the presence of some prominent dignitaries: Britain's Under-Secretary of State at the Department of Transport, Jim Fitzpatrick, witnessed the event, while Italy even mustered her Prime Minister to attend the scene. The Italian flag was lowered at 1100 and the Red Ensign raised. There was a thorough Britishness to the event – enhanced by the presence of the Band of the Scots Guards, which performed on board for the numerous guests of honour.

After final preparations *Queen Victoria* left her 'birthplace', and a course was set for Southampton, where the vessel arrived a week later. Befittingly the city had set up a large

programme of events to celebrate the arrival of
Britain's youngest addition to the merchant
fleet, the highlight being the naming ceremony
on 10 December 2007. Again a large provisional
auditorium, seating 2,000, had been set up, but
in a different spot: The christening of the *Queen
Victoria* did not take place in the traditional
Ocean Dock, but at the City Cruise Terminal.
With modern security regulations banning
visitors from entering the harbour, this ensured
much better visibility for spectators, as
Southampton's Mayflower Park was nearby.
And, as with the *QM2* four years previously,
large video screens were set up.

Adding to the glitz of the day, the sun shone
brilliantly from a cloudless sky when HRH the
Duchess of Cornwall, accompanied by HRH the
Prince of Wales, boarded the *Queen Victoria* on
the big day. The royal visitors were given the
customary tour of the vessel, and on the bridge
the Duchess was given the honour to sound the
whistle, just as her consort had done when the
QE2 had first left her builder's yard thirty-nine

years previously.

The naming ceremony was to be the apogee
of the day, but took a rather inauspicious turn at
its high point. Speeches and musical
performances went ahead as could be expected at
a high-class event such as the naming of a new
Cunarder. And eventually Captain Paul Wright
asked Her Royal Highness to step on the stage
and perform the christening. And so the
Duchess of Cornwall said the traditional words:
'I name this ship *Queen Victoria*. May God bless
her and all who sail in her' and pressed the
button that was to release a bottle of Veuve
Cliquot Champagne.

The mechanism worked as planned and hit
the bottle against the ship's side – and it failed to
break! One can only assume that many a
spectator must have gasped, and Cunard officials
must have been horrified.

It is not known whether the bottle had been
filed, as had been the case with the *QM2*. On
the other hand perhaps it would not have been a
proper christening of a Cunard Queen had all

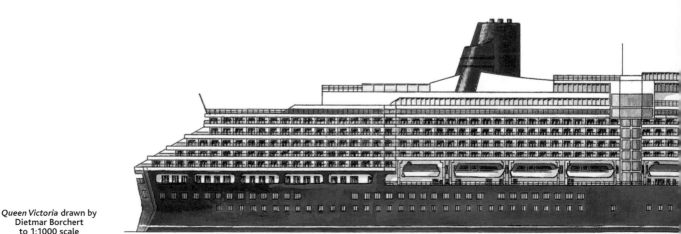

Queen Victoria drawn by
Dietmar Borchert
to 1:1000 scale

Hamburg was one of the
ports of call on the inaugural
voyage

KAI ORTEL

A Scandinavian welcome

MARTIN GRANT

Route of the maiden voyage
in December 2007

CUNARD

gone well. In 1934, seconds after HM Queen Mary had named the then new Cunarder, a forgetful shipyard employee had failed to switch off the microphone which had broadcast Her Majesty's words on radio. And so all over the country, people could hear her address to the yard's officials: 'And now I press the button?'

Four years later the microphone was not switched on at all when HM Queen Elizabeth named the next great Cunarder, and so spectators were led to believe that the launching had gone ahead without a blessing. And as we have seen in a previous chapter, the *Queen Elizabeth 2* was not to have had that name at all.

On a positive note it may be added that at least the bottle of Prosecco, smashed against the ship's side by *madrina* Maureen Ryan, had splintered charmingly. Distracting everybody present from this little hiccup, a firework lit up the sky after the naming, and a great reception was held aboard the vessel.

The following day, *Queen Victoria*'s career began in earnest when she set sail on her maiden voyage to Rotterdam, Copenhagen, Oslo, Hamburg and Zeebrugge. Among the lucky ones having a cabin on the vessel's first voyage were the celebrated maritime historian John Maxtone-Graham and his wife, Mary. And as the author I am greatly honoured to be able to

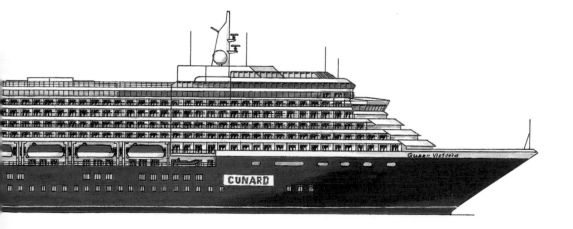

add here some first-hand impressions that he has contributed about life on board during the maiden voyage:

To anyone even remotely connected to the cruise industry, an invitation to attend the christening and maiden voyage of a new Cunarder is a gratifying privilege. First of all, an honour to be

A passageway runs along the Café Carinthia, giving it the air of a boardwalk café

MARTIN GRANT

among those gathering for the ceremony, especially one featuring a member of the Royal Family, coupled with the sense of excitement, anticipation and privilege inevitably connected to every gleaming new building.

Then too, the cruise industry is, after all is said and done, a rather small and selective world. At every christening I am struck by the number of old friends, not seen since the previous christening (*Queen Mary 2* in 2004) who assemble once again. One finds one's cabin, changes into evening dress and decorations and gathers at an assigned table in the dining room for a superb dinner. There are not only old friends throughout the room, there are also old friends among the staff: Pio, now a captain in *Queen Victoria*'s dining room, was one of our

original trio of stewards in the Queen's Grill aboard QM2; and once the maiden voyage began, as Mary and I took our seats at our customary table for two, Mehmet, a luncheon steward last summer aboard *Queen Mary 2*'s three transatlantics last June, appeared, smiling, at our elbow.

There are dozens of initial impressions gathered when one is a maiden voyage passenger rather than merely an overnight visitor. Shipboard's community coalesces as it only can at sea and the long-awaited departure from Southampton was enriched by a superb fireworks display just off the terminal. Then we set off down Southampton Water bound for Spithead and the sea.

It was a short overnight passage to Rotterdam, where our path crossed with homebound *Queen Elizabeth 2*, tied up in the port some distance away. Despite that distance, we played host to scores of curious QE2 crewmen and women who came over to inspect the new Cunarder. One fortuitous visitor encountered as we lunched in the Lido was Gregory, one of *QE2*'s Queen's Grill maîtres d'hôtel. Thanks to that chance meeting, we could book our (regular) Queen's Grill table #52 for our final voyage aboard the vessel next August.

One common affliction suffered by all passengers and crew at every port was the penetration into the ship's interiors of brisk seasonal weather. Although plainly advertised as [a] Christmas Market cruise, none of us had anticipated the bone-chilling cold that infused the vessel throughout every port day. Decks 1, 2 and 3 were essentially open to the outside. The winter damp of Rotterdam, the penetrating cold of Oslo, the wintry intrusion of Copenhagen, the wind-whipped Hamburg littoral and the foggy chill of Zeebrugge characterised every stop.

Most hard-hit were the poor security men and women manning gangways, whether exit or entrance, bundled up as best they could against the bitter, day-long cold. The Grand Lobby shared the chill, and personnel behind the purser's desk wore their warmest clothing as well. The chill's only advantage? Lines at the purser's desk

A section of the Queens Room. Note that it is the maiden voyage, and thus Christmas is near

AUTHOR

were noticeably minimised.

Countering that winter intrusion was the incredible decorative warmth of the public rooms. *Queen Victoria* is no clone of either *QE2* or *QM2* but her own distinctive vessel. There is a preponderance of mahogany coloured panelling throughout, pleasantly patterned but not over-busy carpeting, extremely deft curtains and window treatments and overall, a distinctive art deco look incorporated by the vessel's two major designers, Giacomo Mortola and Teresa Anderson. I was especially taken by the pleasing balconied overviews above not only the Grand Lobby but also the Queens Room further aft. The vessel works well, the flow between public rooms is manageable and the Victorian 'music hall' theatre a delight, complete with its selection of boxes and corridor approaches reminiscent of London's Drury Lane.

For the dedicated ship buff there is a plentitude – perhaps too much? – of Cunard history in the form of paintings, ephemera, posters and models. Canvases by Robert Lloyd, Stephen Card and Gordon Bauwens abound in every lounge, stairwell and corridor; Lloyd's evocative 'Britannia' and 'Servia' at the after end of the Chart Room are absolutely superb.

All in all, a vessel to be remembered well and pleasingly, one that I shall see work again in normal sea-going mode this coming January as we cross to New York. Port-rich, northern winter cruises are all very well, but the real test of any Cunarder will come as we embark across that notoriously unpredictable ocean arena, Winter North Atlantic.

Due to the season the in-port events were a bit more low key compared with the spectacular

The theatre aboard *Queen Victoria* is the first to have private boxes

CUNARD

external appearance.

But apart from this she was much acclaimed for the beautiful, and indeed very comfortable, decoration of her public rooms. Passengers found that the profusion of wood and marble (both artificial, of course) and soft cushions made for a very warm, welcoming 'country house' atmosphere which very well suited her target British market. Moreover, compared with the *QM2*, her public rooms were smaller and had a more human and less daunting feel to them.

Finally, and probably most importantly, given that it was a maiden voyage, there were very few problems – only some faults with toilet flushes; and the doors to the Winter Garden would not shut (so the room was permanently freezing). But the meals in the main dining room were served promptly and reliably.

The maiden voyage was followed by a sixteen-night Christmas and New Year's cruise to the Canary Islands, and it was during this voyage that the press found its proof that an unsmashed bottle at a ship's christening is a bad omen. During the cruise seventy-eight passengers were infected with the Norovirus, but fortunately all recovered within a few days, and despite small headlines the incident was soon forgotten.

These two voyages could be seen as the 'shakedown' to *Queen Victoria*'s first world cruise. The departure coincided with that of the *QE2* on her last-ever world cruise, and so the two vessels sailed from Southampton on 6 January 2008 on a spectacular tandem transatlantic crossing. Let us hear a few more impressions by John Maxtone-Graham:

We had two gale-filled days once clear of the Channel and buried our bow a couple of times; so did *QE2*. But she handled the weather well. It was all pitching with no rolling; in fact, Captain Paul Wright told me that he never once, throughout the crossing, deployed the vessel's stabilisers.

The real delight was sailing in tandem with

welcomes on the *QM2*'s inaugural voyage (or season for that matter), but all agreed that especially Southampton and, once again, Hamburg made the effort of spectacular send-offs when the ship sailed; and the vessel received very favourable critiques from her passengers.

One of the most detailed points of criticism was stowage space in the cabins. Again compared with the *QM2*, the cabins were nowhere near as lavishly appointed – no sophisticated in-cabin TV system, no bathroom storage space and very little drawer space. Apparently, the reason for this was that Cunard copied the cabin specification used by the Holland America Vista Class ships, which are primarily designed for seven-to-ten-day informal warm-weather cruises when not many clothes are required. A second point on which *Queen Victoria* fell second best behind her illustrious predecessors was her

QE2, something I have never done before. The continuing sight of *QE2*, doubly evocative because she is so near to permanent Dubai retirement, was really marvellous. The Masters of the vessels kept them close but not too close and changed sides daily to give photographers aboard both vessels a chance with the sun. It is hard to describe the feeling of seeing her night and day just off either side. She was a kind of benign Flying Dutchman, a marvellous *doppelgänger* always there and a vision that delighted everyone on board, crew and passengers alike. Of course, it was a field day for

the buffs, but even little old ladies sat entranced and transfixed by the windows on Deck 3, gazing at our accompanying fleet-mate for hours at a time. And of course, every change of photograph was rung – through a QV life-ring or merely just over our rail. There was one Grand Banks day when *QE2*'s hull disappeared into some surface fog so that only her upper works were visible, an eerie sight.

Overall, a great crossing, particularly since I had some of my family with us and there were so many chums on board.

On 13 January the venerable ocean liner and her youthful consort arrived in New York City to a big celebration – and a solitary 'family reunion' with their larger fleet-mate *Queen Mary 2* – and against the backdrop of Manhattan Island, the Statue of Liberty and a gigantic fireworks display the three heirs to the Cunard tradition sailed on the respective world cruises in the evening of that day.

At the time of writing the next stage of the story exists only in prediction. It will be exciting to see how the *Queen Victoria* – the first Cunard Queen to be a cruise ship and not a liner – will find her place in the fleet. So far no life expectancy has been stated officially for her. Will she still be sailing the seven seas in forty years, in 2047, as is planned for *QM2*? During this

period will she be subjected to major changes yet remain herself, as did the illustrious *QE2*? Will she still be wearing the classic livery of the Cunard Line?

The difference between *Queen Victoria* and her two existing sisters is not minor. As full-blooded liners, *QE2* and *QM2* personify the Cunard Line. Which other undertaking can claim to be *the* transatlantic shipping company? On the other hand, *Queen Victoria* with her different livery and funnel could be confused quite easily with another 'brand' of the Carnival Corporation, as the case of the *Arcadia* shows.

Looking ahead a little, it is easy to imagine how the days aboard *Queen Victoria* will be just as 'ship-lagged' and the nights as unforgettable as those which countless enchanted passengers aboard *QE2* or *QM2* have already experienced. And so it may be right and proper to conclude this chapter with a little tour aboard the *Queen Victoria*.

Coming aboard, a passenger's first impression will be of the spectacular Grand Lobby that, as on the *QM2*, serves as an entrance hall and focal point of shipboard life. The Atrium reaches up three levels. The lower level houses only the Purser's Desk and the Internet Centre. The central eye-catcher is the broad staircase with its mahogany and brass rails, undoubtedly inspired by the First-Class passengers' staircase of the White Star Line's *Olympic*. On the landing is an archway two and a half decks high containing a bronze relief by John McKenna, a fresh interpretation of the historical story portrayed aboard the first *Queen Mary*. Here the *Queen Victoria* is set against a compass-rose on a map of the North Atlantic. Galleries with glass balustrades on either side of the Grand Lobby complete the middle and upper levels. A large area of public rooms occupies these two decks so that there is constant foot traffic to and fro, surely of interest to the quiet observers who have made themselves comfortable in the armchairs and sofas in the lower-level vestibule.

The Royal Arcade is a 'shopping mall' in Victorian retro-style

CUNARD

A maiden voyage in the North Sea in December may not have inspired everybody to rise at dawn for a constitutional along the wide Promenade Deck at Deck 10 level, but anything is possible in calm weather with some sunshine. After a few deep breaths one comes alive, and the sunny Lido Restaurant a deck lower offers an opulent breakfast buffet. Provided that the ship will spend all day at sea, after breakfast all diversions and pastimes proceed as with our

Atlantic voyage aboard *QM2*. Memento-hunters will first review the photo gallery on Deck 3 for pictures of the boarding at Southampton or the Captain's reception the previous evening and then head for the foreship to visit the Royal Arcade, the shopping centre of the ship. The shops' façades are of wood, the windows leaded. An opening in the deck, lined by cast-iron rails, reveals a view of the casino on the deck below.

Whereas the *QM2* was made distinctive with

Another version of the
famous *QE2* smoke uptake.
Note that the wind deflector
of the *Queen Victoria*'s
funnel does not serve as
such

MARTIN GRANT

art deco furbishing, the *Queen Victoria* designers used the Victorian era for their theme. The Royal Arcade is intended to reproduce its nineteenth-century London namesake, a very early forerunner of our modern shopping centres. Not least the carpeting and mock historic gas lamps contribute to this impression. Mid-morning refreshment after the bustle of shopping can be found by descending the curvaceous double stairway at the forward end of

the Royal Arcade into the Golden Lion Pub. Deck 2 contains the Library with around 6,000 volumes. Dark wooden furniture, frosted glass in the bookcase doors, a winding staircase joining the two levels of the Library, green leather armchairs and a glass, Tiffany-style dome overhead give the place a nineteenth-century London feel.

The morning has flown by, and for lunch passengers of the higher cabin categories repair to the exquisite Queen's Grill or Princess Grill. These two prime restaurants are on Deck 11 at the foot of the funnel and are the last remnants of class division. Only the guests of these restaurants have access to the lofty sun terrace above. More interesting is the Courtyard, a patio between the two grills in which, in warmer climates, one may dine alfresco protected from the wind. A decorated fountain provides a little Mediterranean flair. So high up in the ship her pitching movement will be felt most strongly here, and sensitive guests will wish that a set of stabilisers had been installed in the vertical axis as well as the horizontal. After eating, *Queen Victoria* passengers who have overdone the calories may wish to proceed to Deck 9 directly abaft the bridge, where the Cunard Health Club and Spa is situated. After a spell working out on

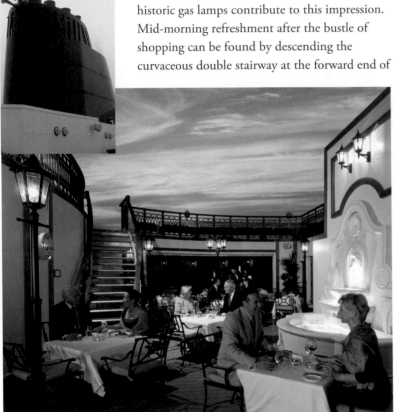

The courtyard at the foot of the funnel

CUNARD

Cunardia is probably the first, albeit small, museum on the high seas.

CUNARD

The Commodore Club aboard *Queen Victoria* differs considerably from its counterpart on board the *QM2*

CUNARD LINE

the exercise machines, one may have a massage, and then do a few lengths below the glass roof of the neighbouring Pavilion Pool. Conscience assuaged, the passenger could then proceed astern for afternoon tea with scones and clotted cream and delicate sandwich triangles in the Winter Garden. Guests less concerned with food might feel the need at midday for some cultural enlightenment and visit Cunardia, probably the first museum aboard a seagoing ship. Original artefacts from Cunard's long history are displayed here.

The shorter days of December will afford guests at the first sitting in the Britannia Restaurant the opportunity to watch the sunset

The Cunard Health Club & Spa

CUNARD LINE

The Britannia Restaurant extends over two decks

CUNARD

Large windows and potted plants make the bridge a cosy place

ROSMARY SCHWERDTNER

with an aperitif. Hemispheres is a panoramic room on Deck 10 offering a 270-degree view over decks and sea which during the day will be used for lectures and courses, becoming a night-club at night. The Commodore Club has a view over the (short) forecastle and sea and will be equally appreciated for a drink and relaxation. It is located on Deck 10 at the forward end of the superstructure, one deck above the bridge. While its counterpart on *QM2* offers a friendly and modern atmosphere, guests of the Commodore Club aboard *Queen Victoria* may imagine themselves taken back in time to a British gentlemen's club of the Victorian era with its high-backed armchairs, leather sofas, brass balustrades, mahogany trimmings and card tables. One will be served a fine Scotch whisky here.

The high point of the day at sea is the evening programme, beginning with dinner in the Britannia Restaurant. Glass and bronze dominate in this dining room of two decks' height. It has a fine wall relief, a globe against the outline of the Atlantic Ocean, and depicts the great era of the British Empire. In the lower corner the silhouette of an English town with

smoking factory chimneys indicates the period, all being lit by the ray of the sun in the left hand corner. After dinner the evening entertainment begins, from the West End Show in the Royal Court Theatre (the first at sea to have private boxes) to dancing in the Queens Room; from the karaoke party in the Golden Lion Pub to a glass of champagne for two in the Champagne

Queen Victoria at the outset of what one hopes will be a long and successful career

SERGIO DE LUYK

Bar, perhaps to celebrate an anniversary; from a conversation with newly-won friends in the Chart Room to a cigar in Churchill's Cigar Lounge: the variety of opportunities for passing the time are as numerous as the public rooms aboard the *Queen Victoria*, and without doubt there will be 'night-owls' among the passengers of the newest Cunarder who will celebrate into the early hours.

Whichever harbours the *Queen Victoria* may steer towards over the years ahead as the standard-bearer in the tradition of her forerunners, she will receive due deference, perhaps more than many other contemporary and even larger cruise ships. May she have a long and varied career, and always enjoy plain sailing!

CAPTAIN PAUL WRIGHT INTERVIEW

On 6 October 2006 Cunard announced in a press release that Captain Paul Wright, who had been transferred to *Diamond Princess* in June 2005, had been appointed the first Master of *Queen Victoria*. This fifty-eight-year-old seaman began his officer apprenticeship in 1965 aboard a Shell tanker before serving for the first time on a passenger ship with Canadian Pacific in 1969. Cunard could scarcely have made a better choice for the role: loved by passengers and crew, he is not only a highly qualified officer but also a true gentleman of the old school. His public appearances and talks are always conversation points and therefore well attended.

Q What ships have you sailed on?

A Since I joined Cunard in 1980 I have sailed on the *Cunard Countess*, *Cunard Princess*, *Sagafjord*, *Cunard Crown Dynasty*, *QE2*, *QM2*. Prior to Cunard I spent many years on container ships, tankers, general cargo, hovercraft and ferries.

Q Which did you cherish the most?

A I have enjoyed aspects and my time on of all of them. I don't think I can single out a specific ship.

Q Where do you feel at home?

A I am a citizen of the world and the Seven Seas. I am very adaptable and can really feel at home anywhere either ashore or afloat. My main residence is in Cornwall.

Q You share the helm of a ship with a relief Master. What do you do the other half of the year?

A It is actually less than half a year at home, more like five months. In my spare time I enjoy sailing my own twenty-nine-foot yacht in Cornwall – which is a beautiful area of the world. I also enjoy gardening and fixing things. I used to do a lot of scuba diving in the years past and especially enjoyed wreck diving.

Q When you return home on holidays do you have to get accustomed to things, as everyday life has moved on in your

absence, or are you at home from day one?

A It always takes a while for a sailor to adapt to going home, just like it takes a while to adapt to being back at sea after a period of leave. I hate arriving home to the piles of mail after being away for three months.

Q What is the difference between the *Queen Mary 2* and the new *Queen Victoria*?

A Obviously size, for one. I have no doubt that the *Queen Victoria* will become an extremely popular ship with very exciting itineraries. She will have all the facilities and ambience that passengers associate with Cunard. Although obviously not as fast as *QM2* – she will of course be Panamax and dock in ports that the larger ships cannot.

Q And the *Queen Elizabeth 2*?

A A classic! She still commands an extraordinary amount of loyalty. *Queen Victoria* will of course be much more manoeuvrable than the *QE2* and hence not reliant on tug availability. I am very happy that a new home has been found for her with an entity willing to invest money in her. This way people will be able to enjoy her for many years to come. I may even visit myself some time in the future.

Q Would you see the *Queen Victoria* as a

true successor to the classic Cunard ocean liners (notably the Queens), or is it just another cruise liner?

A I see the *Queen Victoria* as being a true Cunarder which has the advantage of the most modern technology, facilities and outstanding service which will attract both passengers who have consistently sailed with Cunard and those who haven't yet tried Cunard but like new ships and the size. I see it as filling a gap in the Cunard fleet.

Q Along with Commodore Warwick you have been one of the first captains of the *Queen Mary 2*. How did you feel when you were appointed Master of the *Queen Mary 2*?

A Ecstatic!

Q And for the *Queen Victoria*?

A Ecstatic!

Q You claim that the *Queen Mary 2*'s maiden arrival in Hamburg was one of your most memorable moments at sea. Would you like to share some insight on this occasion with us?

A I think there is absolutely no doubt that Hamburg's welcome to *QM2* was absolutely magnificent and most certainly the highlight of my career at sea. Hamburg's love of ships was overwhelmingly evident both on our transit to and arrival and stay in Hamburg. I don't think anyone onboard could have even imagined the welcome we were to receive. Thank you Hamburg!

Q Do you have any other relations to Hamburg or Germany?

A Unfortunately not, but it's one of my favourite ports in the whole world.

Q Why was the *Queen Mary 2* equipped with quadruple screws when most other passenger ships nowadays have only two?

A She has two fixed pods and two azimuthing pods. She needs all those to obtain her top speed.

Q The *Queen Mary 2* is equipped with gas turbines to attain her top speed. But as she is usually sailing below that, are the turbines used at all?

A One of the advantages of *QM2* is her speed, and hence she offers itineraries that other ships cannot. She uses one or both of her gas turbines frequently to obtain the speed to carry out these itineraries. On transatlantic the turbines are used to maintain scheduled arrival times and especially when Atlantic adverse weather systems make it prudent to avoid these, which will increase the distance and hence the speed required. She will therefore have speed in hand for both weather considerations and also routine engine maintenance. So to answer your question yes, she does engage her gas turbines regularly.

Q Two of the four azipods are fixed in position whereas the other two are azimuthing. Does that mean the azipods are interchangeable only in pairs, or could theoretically one of the fixed pods be used to replace a damaged azimuthing pod?

A No, as far as I am aware a fixed pod is not interchangeable with an azimuthing pod.

Q Early photographs of the *Queen Mary 2* often show the top of her bulbous bow out of the water, even allowing a man to stand on it in a Caribbean port. Later pictures show the bulbous bow always completely submerged. What is the reason behind this?

A Ideally the bulbous bow should be submerged whenever possible, but depending on status of fuel bunkers, ballast, freshwater and stability considerations it is not always possible.

Q How come officers are now being swapped between the Carnival companies?

A When Princess assumed the management of Cunard the intention was to share best practices from both companies, and obviously the best way to do this was to expose officers to the existing practices in both fleets.

Q How do you feel about being back with Cunard?

A As of writing this I am presently sailing in command of the *Diamond Princess* in Alaska. I return to Cunard in November and am very much looking forward to it

Q Do you feel more like a Cunard or a Carnival officer?

A Cunard.

Q In Cunard as a company, is there still anything to be felt of the company's long tradition?

A Yes, I can say that without hesitation or doubt.

Q How much American influence is there on shipboard life and anything 'typically British'?

A Carnival has always been very careful not to change the individual 'brands' under their umbrella. It's an international company which offers a wide range of cruising styles and ambience, and this policy of not changing the styles of its different cruise lines has undoubtedly contributed to its success.

Q What kind of clientele do you think Cunard will focus on in the future?

A That's a question you would have to ask our marketing people but I am sure they would say 'everyone!'

Q What do you think of the continuous growth of cruise ships?

A Guess it has proven the popularity of cruising. I am sure when I retire I will take a cruise. It's safe, affordable and excellent value.

Q What do you think about the international concentration of cruise lines in the hands of a few large companies?

A I think it keeps the prices of cruising down because of synergies and bargaining power for the multitude of services and supplies cruise ships need to operate.

Q Could you imagine the *Queen Mary 2* being used in a similar capacity as the *QE2* during the Falklands Conflict?

A Although she would undoubtedly be capable, I hope indeed similar circumstances never arise.

Q If you could travel through time and chose to travel on any particular ocean liner of the past, which one would you chose?

A *Queen Mary*.

Q As a passenger, or as Master?

A As Master of course!

7

FAREWELL *QE2*!

QE2 in her home port of
Southampton. Soon she will
have a new home in Dubai

AUTHOR

'When the *QE2* became the longest-serving Cunarder of all time on 4 September 2005, after thirty-six years, four months and three days in commission since her maiden voyage, technical circles began to ask how much longer the old liner could keep sailing the seas of the world. Although there had been ships before *QE2* with longer lives, and few ships of her age had kept their youth so well, a look at the figures was enough to prove that the liner had long outlived her life expectancy. Cunard made it clear that it did not intend to decommission *QE2* in the foreseeable future and that as she conformed to the new SOLAS regulations she could continue in service beyond 2010. Purely financial grounds dictated that the last years of her long sea career were almost through, however. *QE2* had been in service longer with her 'new' main engines than with the original steam turbines. Technical developments had overtaken these in many respects, and in the light of the trend towards

Villas along a 'branch' of The Palm Jumeirah

NAKHEEL

The Palm Jumeirah, March 2007

NAKHEEL

surprise even in technical circles. It had been assumed that Cunard would hold back with such an announcement until at least the introduction of *Queen Victoria*.

The future disposition of the ship came as a surprise: the state-owned Dubai investment firm Istithmar had acquired the liner for $100 million. Cunard announced that the *QE2* would be delivered to the Arab state in November 2008

fleets of newer ships it was certain that time was running out. It is assumed that *QE2* was kept going so long because the Carnival Corporation's marketing policy gave her a fresh injection of life. The principal business aim of a shipping line, however, is to earn money by operating ships, and to run a vessel like the *QE2* at a loss out of pure nostalgia would be foolhardy.

It was no secret that a Southampton business consortium had long been interested in acquiring *QE2* for use as a hotel ship and museum once she was decommissioned. When Cunard announced the sale of its long-serving flagship on 18 June 2007, the report caused

to become part of 'The Palm Jumeirah' beach complex. The largest artificial island in the world, it stems from the vision of the former Prime Minister of the United Arab Emirates Sheikh Mohammed bin Rashid Al Maktoum. By the beginning of the 1990s oil had made the Emirates rich, but the reserves were not inexhaustible. What else did the country have to offer the world? Almost guaranteed sunshine and white beaches. The Sheikh's idea was to turn the country, or rather the Dubai Emirate, in which 99 per cent of the social life of the UAE takes place, into one of the most important tourist destinations in the world. Subsequently the state holding company Dubai World was founded to

**QE2 at the end of her long
and successful career**

CUNARD

'Nakheel'). The first Palm, The Palm Jumeirah, was begun in 2002, and although the complex is not yet complete, numerous luxury villas are already occupied. Istithmar (Arabic: investment) is the purchasing company of Dubai World and therefore Cunard's contract partner in the sale of the *QE2*. The liner will be moved to a pier at the Palm Jumeirah built expressly for the purpose, the press bulletin continued, to serve as a floating hotel, museum and shopping mall.

One has to see these Dubai islands to imagine at what cost a whole city has been implanted upon the sea. Almost 2.5 square miles were reclaimed for the Palm Jumeirah project. Seven million tons of rock and 3.3 billion cubic feet of sand were removed, enough to build a wall twenty feet high and twenty inches thick and long enough to circle the world. The investment of a sum of over $3 billion not only hints at the wealth of the Dubai Emirate, but suggests that the payment for the *QE2* could have come from petty cash. Even so, for Cunard the return was presumably far more than ever it could have expected for the old liner.

'We are delighted,' the Cunard President Carol Marlow explained, 'that when her legendary career as an ocean liner ends there will continue to be a permanent home for her that will enable future generations to continue to experience fully both the ship and her history.' Sultan Ahmed bin Sulayem, Chairman of Dubai World, added:

concentrate all activities for the expansion of tourism. An important aim was the artificial extension of the forty-mile-long Dubai coastline. For this purpose the project-development firm Nakheel (Arabic: palms) was founded and given the job of extending the coast by creating several artificial island groups in the thirty-three-foot deeps off Dubai. In probably no other country of the world have there been so many forward-looking projects as in Dubai. Among the sixteen projects which Nakheel has developed to date, with a budget exceeding $30 billion, are the island group 'The World', which seen from the air resembles a map of the world, and three island groups in the shape of palms (hence the name

QE2 is without a doubt one of the wonders of the maritime world, and is easily the most famous serving liner in the world today. I am delighted we will be able to create a home for her on the newest wonder of the world, The Palm Jumeirah. *QE2* at The Palm Jumeirah will become one of the must-see experiences of Dubai and of the Middle East. We are investing in creating a truly global tourism destination. Dubai is a maritime nation and we understand the rich heritage of *QE2*. She is coming to a home where she will be cherished.

He went on to say that the renovation of the ship will retain all original fittings except the casino. Gambling is illegal in Dubai.

The report of the sale of *QE2* came as a bombshell internationally. Around the world the liner hit the headlines of newspapers large and small. Some provided no more than the sober announcement that the ship had been sold, while others were more flowery, such as *The Scotsman*'s 'Ship of the Desert'. Others of note were 'Today one of our greatest post-war ships ... tomorrow a hotel' (*The Herald*), and '*QE2* says Du-Bye to Cruising' (*The Daily Record*). Worldwide these headlines provided a diverse but emotional echo. The end of the *QE2*'s career left a bittersweet after-taste in some quarters. Devotees lamented that she would no longer sail the world's oceans while others were satisfied in the knowledge that she was to be

Eighty-eight-year-old Beatrice Muller, an American, is the only permanent inhabitant of *QE2*. On her first world cruise in 1995 she fell in love with the ship and repeated the cruise every year. After the death of her husband aboard she decided to return, calculating that her pension would go equally far living in a small cabin aboard *QE2*. The service would be better, and she would be constantly meeting new people while seeing the world. In January 2000 'Bea' Muller moved into the ship, and apart from occasional visits to her children in New Jersey she has remained aboard. When asked if she would try to find another berth or 'swallow the anchor' she replied:

'The news about *QE2*'s being sold to Dubai for a luxury hotel in November of 2008 will make quite a change in my life. It is sad to lose my precious home yet we are all so grateful that her charm and graciousness will be preserved. So often ships are scrapped when they have finished their sailing lives.

'Now since I must find a new home at sea I'm looking forward to the reports on the *Queen Victoria* when she begins her life at the end of this year. I have sailed on the *QE2*, off and on, alone and with my family for more than twelve years now and am utterly spoiled as you can well imagine. There will never be another great liner like *Queen Elizabeth 2*. How we will miss her!'

spared the fate of *Norway* ex-*France*, another great transatlantic liner, which the year before had been run aground off the Indian town of Alang prior to breaking.

At Southampton there was heated debate as to why city officials had not taken a stand against the sale of this piece of British and municipal history. Whereas such emotions are understandable, all parties aim to recoup their investments and the Southampton city council considered it doubtful that they could recover the £50 million needed to buy the ship, and felt that the money would be better invested in schools and road construction.

Two days after announcing the sale, Cunard cancelled two Mediterranean cruises, a tour of Biscay and a cruise to the Canaries scheduled for the autumn of 2008, replacing them with a number of farewell voyages. Passengers already booked were offered a full refund or a re-booking for one of the replacement voyages on specially favourable terms, such as a $300 voucher for shipboard purchases. These four voyages included (i) a ten-day cruise around the British Isles calling at the former Irish transatlantic port of Cobh, making visits for the first and last time to Dublin and Belfast and also calling at Liverpool, Greenock, near the yard on the Clyde where *QE2* was built, then Edinburgh and Newcastle; and a transatlantic passage in tandem with *QM2* (ii and iii) so that *QE2* could take her leave of her US station at New York and run the transatlantic route for the last time. The final departure from New York would be her 806th. The final voyage (iv) was the sixteen-day 'Voyage to Dubai', delivering the ship to her new home via the Mediterranean and the Suez Canal. As great demand was expected for these voyages, bookings worldwide were made available from 1500 hours Central European Time on 27 June 2007. The Dubai voyage was sold out in thirty-six minutes.

The next announcement from Cunard was

The decision to order another ship for Cunard Line has been taken as a result of the strong booking response to the new *Queen Victoria,* and we are extremely pleased that Cunard will once again become a three-ship fleet so soon after the departure of the much-celebrated *Queen Elizabeth 2* in November next year. Furthermore we are delighted that Her Majesty the Queen has given her blessing to our calling this new Cunarder *Queen Elizabeth*, after our first vessel of that name.

The only information given was that the *Queen Elizabeth* would be a ship of 92,000 gross tons (thus strongly pointing at an updated Vista Class vessel) for 2,092 passengers that will have its home port in Southampton. The building cost was given at 500 million euros.

Subsequently Cunard must have been swamped with booking requests, letters and e-mails from aficionados on the hunt for more information, as a few weeks later the press release was augmented by the following two sentences: 'Details of *Queen Elizabeth*'s itineraries for her maiden season are currently being finalised and no reservations or waitlists are being taken at this time. Further details of *Queen Elizabeth* and her maiden season will be released in due course, in the meantime we thank you for your patience.'

At the time of writing it remains to be seen where in the rich history of the Cunard Line the new *Queen Elizabeth* will find her place.

For the *QE2* a further chapter in her long life will come to an end just as with the old *Queen Mary*, which ended her sea wanderings at Long Beach in 1967. The latter has fulfilled her 'new' role longer than her time as an ocean liner, and despite all predictions to the contrary her end is not in sight. The desert climate of Dubai will be less adverse for *QE2*, and while Dubai has a surplus of money, her upkeep seems assured. No Cunard ship has spent more hours at sea per year than *QE2*. She has earned a rest.

In September 2007 the *QE2* celebrated her 40th birthday with a special theme cruise. Anniversary banners adorn the Queens Room

MARTIN GRANT

The vessel even received a birthday cake

MARTIN GRANT

not long in following: On 10 October 2007 the Line surprised experts and fans alike with the news that a new vessel had been ordered from Fincantieri for delivery in 2010. And if aficionados had hitherto been sure there would never be a third *Queen Elizabeth* – for QE3 just sounded too awful to their ears – the press release stated that the new ship would be named just that: *Queen Elizabeth* (but without even a number in arabic).

While the news item carried little information about the intended use of the ship and consisted mostly of corporate speak, Carol Marlow was quoted as saying:

TECHNICAL DATA

	Queen Mary	*Queen Elizabeth*	*Queen Elizabeth 2*	*Queen Elizabeth 2* (after change of engines)	*Queen Mary 2*	*Queen Victoria*
Builder's yard	John Brown & Co, Clydebank	John Brown & Co, Clydebank	John Brown & Co, Clydebank	Lloyd Werft, Bremerhaven	ALSTOM – Chantiers de l'Atlantique, St-Nazaire	Fincantieri Cantieri Navali, Marghera
Yard number	534	552	736	—	G32	6127
Cost of construction	£4.5 million	£5 million	£29.1 million	£180 million	£550 million	£300 million
Keel laid	27 December 1930	6 December 1936	5 July 1965	—	4 July 2002	16 May 2006
Date launched or set afloat	26 September 1934	27 September 1938	20 September 1967	—	20 March 2003	15 January 2007
Ceremonial naming by	HM Queen Mary, consort of King George V	HM Queen Elizabeth, consort of I King George V	HM Queen Elizabeth II	—	HM Queen Elizabeth II	HRH The Duchess of Cornwall
Maiden voyage	27 May 1936	2 March 1940	2 May 1969	29 April 1987	12 January 2004	10 December 2007
Tonnage	81,237 gross tons	83,673 gross tons	65,863 gross tons	66,450 gross tons	148,528 gross tons	90,000 gross tons
Length	975.20ft	1,031.00ft	963.00ft	—	1,131.89ft	964.50ft
Width	118.60ft	118.60ft	105.30ft	—	134.51ft	106.00ft
Draught	39.37ft	39.37ft	32.80ft	—	32.80ft	26.20ft
Top speed	32 knots	over 30 knots	32.66 knots	34.6 knots	30 knots	23.7 knots
Main engines	4 sets of geared turbines	4 sets of geared turbines	2 sets of geared turbines	9 MAN-B&W 9-cylinder diesels	4 Wärtsilä 16V46C-CR diesels	4 Wärtsilä-Sulzer ZA40 diesels
Propulsion	4 propellers	4 propellers	2 propellers	2 General Electric 44MW	4 Rolls-Royce 21.5MW drive motors	2 ABB 17.6MW Azipods Mermaid pods
Engine output	160,000hp	160,000hp	110,000hp	130,000hp	160,000hp	103,000hp
Passenger decks	12	12	13	14	13	12
Passenger capacity	2,038	2,260	2,025	1,877	2,620	2,014
Number of crew	1,285	1,296	906	—	1,238	c900

ACKNOWLEDGEMENTS

Even if there is only a single name on the cover, a book is nevertheless a product towards whose construction and presentation many collaborators lend a hand, some as part of their job, others in friendship. Some sacrifice many hours to ensure that ultimately the result on the bookshelves will be the best possible. With others it will have been small tasks such as the preparation of photographic material. Each of them will have left at least a fingerprint in the finished work. So it is my most pleasant task in the overall writing process as author to thank here all the industrious helpers who gave me support in my work.

First of all I thank my wife Rosy for her patience and tolerance during the occasionally tiring writing phase of this book. During the final months she let me get on with it while she handled both the household and our social contacts. I am deeply indebted. For their hard work and good advice I thank my proofreaders Dietmar Borchert, Holger Friese and Kai Ortel; also Arnold Kludas for his ready ear and good advice, and Rudolf Grimme for permission to reproduce his paintings.

I thank my interview partners Florian Bethke (Sartori & Berger), Norbert Browarczyk (Hamburg Port Authority), Götz von Elbe (Hamburg Waterways Police), Axel Gernert (CJP Hamburg GmbH), Ekkehard Guhn (Hamburg port pilot) and Bernd Spöntjes (Hamburg Waterways Police) for allowing me a little of their time and giving me a highly interesting insight into the conditions under which the special relationship between Hamburg and *QM2* developed. For his Introduction and illustrative material I thank Dr Stefan Behn. I thank Brian O'Connor, Shahram Sadatel and Ingo Thiel (IT-PR GmbH) of Cunard for their help and also Commodore Bernard Warner for the Foreword, and Captain Paul Wright for the interview.

The production of a book involves queries and requests for information on photographic material. For their kind support of this project I am indebted to the following people and companies: Antonio Auterino (Fincantieri), Derek Birkenfield (Rolls-Royce), Ian Boyle (Simplon Postcards), Michael Brasse (ThyssenKrupp Marine Systems/Blohm + Voss), Runhild B. Breivik (Rolls-Royce), Anthony Cooke, Valerio Denaro (www.crocieristi.it), Caterina de Gavardo (Fincantieri), Kjell Göthe (ThyssenKrupp/Kockums), Dirk Heienbrock, David Hutchings, Michael Jackiewicz (Tillberg Design), Fredrik Johannson (Tillberg Design), Milla Johannson (ABB), Nicole Kanner (Regan Communications), Andy Kilk, Jörg Klüver (ThyssenKrupp), Brigitte Krainer, Jukka Kuuskoski (ABB), Mike Lane (Rolls-Royce), Mark Lightowler (designteam), Claes Lindskog (ThyssenKrupp), Kerstin Lotter (Hamburger Hafen und Logistik AG), Sergio de Luyk, Beatrice Muller, Ann-Cathrine Sandas (Wärtsilä Corporation), Jürgen Saupe, Oliver Schmidt, Frank Symeou (designteam), Avril Wilson (Rolls-Royce).

Additionally I wish to extend my thanks to the contributors to the English edition: Martin Grant, John Maxtone-Graham, David Pike and Christoph Walter.

Finally there are those who gave me moral support, either with help or advice or with a ready ear. And here I thank the best friends I could have wished for: Dietmar Borchert, Hamischa Döring, Patrick Hatton, Thorben 'Coxy' Kocks, Dirk Kotte, Carsten Meyer-Mumm, Rolf and Chris Schwerdtner and Hauke Uphues.

In conclusion it remains to be said: 'Nobody is perfect'. Despite all efforts at accuracy we all make mistakes, and so if I have forgotten to mention anybody, it was not intended and I ask for forgiveness.

NILS SCHWERDTNER
May 2008
Queen.project@hamburg.de

BIBLIOGRAPHY

Bonsor, Noel R P, *North Atlantic Seaway* (Vol 1), David & Charles (Holdings) Ltd, Newton Abbot, 1975

—, *North Atlantic Seaway* (Vol 2), Brookside Publications, Jersey, 1978

Butler, Daniel Allen, *The Age of Cunard: A Transatlantic History 1839-2003*, Lighthouse Press, Annapolis, 2003

Hutchings, David F, *Pride of the North Atlantic*, Waterfront / Kingfisher Productions, Settle, 2003

Johnson, Howard, *The Cunard Story*, Whittet Books Ltd, London, 1987

Kludas, Arnold / Heine, Frank / Lose, Frank, *Die großen Passagierschiffe der Welt*, Koehlers Verlagsgesellschaft mbH, Hamburg, 2002

Kludas, Arnold, *Great Passenger Ships of the World: 1951-76*, Patrick Stephens Ltd, Wellingborough, 1976

—, *Great Passenger Ships of the World: 1975-83*, Patrick Stephens Ltd, Wellingborough, 1986

—, *Record Breakers of the North Atlantic: Blue Riband Liners*, Chatham Publishing, London, 1999

Maxtone-Graham, John, Cunard: *150 Glorious Years*, David & Charles Publishers plc, Newton Abbot, 1989

—, *Queen Mary 2: The Greatest Ocean Liner of Our Time*, Bulfinch Press, New York, 2004

Panoff, Bill (Ed), *Cunard Passages 2006*, Panoff Publishing, Inc, Fort Lauderdale, 2005

—, (Ed), *Queen Mary 2*, Panoff Publishing, Inc, Fort Lauderdale, 2003

Payne, Stephen / Knaggs, Tim, *Genesis of a Queen: Cunard Line's Queen Mary 2*, The Royal Institution of Naval Architects, London, 2004

Robinson, Bruce, *Arcadia – A World of New Sensations*, P&O Cruises, Southampton, 2005

Schwerdtner, Nils, *Die Queens des Nordatlantiks*, Koehlers Verlagsgesellschaft mbH, Hamburg, 2003

Wächter, Hans-Christof, *Transatlantische Passage: mit der QE2 in die Neue Welt*, Picus Verlag Ges.m.b.H., Vienna, 2000

PERIODICALS AND OTHER SOURCES

Cunard Line (press releases and promotional materials)

GEO, Gruner + Jahr AG & Co KG, Hamburg

Hamburger Abendblatt, Axel Springer AG, Hamburg

Sea Breezes, Mannin Media Group, Isle of Man

Sea Lines, Ocean Liner Society, London

Ships Monthly, IPC Country and Leisure Media Ltd., Burton-on-Trent

The Southern Daily Echo, Southampton

INTERNET SOURCES

http://www.carnivalcorp.com

http://www.cunard.co.uk

http://www.cunard.com

http://www.cunard.de

http://www.cunardimages.com

http://www.designteam.co.uk

http://www.geae.com

http://www.rolls-royce.com

http://www.thisissouthampton.co.uk

http://www.tillbergdesign.com

http://www.wartsila.com

http://de.wikipedia.org

http://en.wikipedia.org

http://www.seereisen-magazin.de

INDEX